QUANTITATIVE FINANCE FOR PHYSICISTS: AN INTRODUCTION

QUANTITATIVE FINANCE FOR PHYSICISTS: AN INTRODUCTION

ANATOLY B. SCHMIDT

ELSEVIER
ACADEMIC
PRESS

AMSTERDAM • BOSTON • HEIDELBERG • LONDON
NEW YORK • OXFORD • PARIS • SAN DIEGO
SAN FRANCISCO • SINGAPORE • SYDNEY • TOKYO

Elsevier Academic Press
30 Corporate Drive, Suite 400, Burlington, MA 01803, USA
525 B Street, Suite 1900, San Diego, California 92101-4495, USA
84 Theobald's Road, London WC1X 8RR, UK

Library of Congress Cataloging-in-Publication Data
Application submitted.

British Library Cataloguing in Publication Data
A catalogue record for this book is available from the British Library

ISBN: 0-12-088464-X

For all information on all Elsevier Academic Press publications visit our Web site at www.books.elsevier.com

Printed in the United States of America

04 05 06 07 08 09 9 8 7 6 5 4 3 2 1

Table of Contents

Detailed Table of Contents

Chapter 1

Introduction

This book is written for those physicists who want to work on Wall Street but have not bothered to read anything about Finance. This is a crash course that the author, a physicist himself, needed when he landed a financial data analyst job and became fascinated with the huge data sets at his disposal. More broadly, this book addresses the reader with some background in science or engineering (college-level math helps) who is willing to learn the basic concepts and quantitative methods used in modern finance.

The book loosely consists of two parts: the "applied" part and the "academic" one. Two major fields, Econometrics and Mathematical Finance, constitute the applied part of the book. Econometrics can be broadly defined as the methods of model-based statistical inference in financial economics [1]. This book follows the traditional definition of Econometrics that focuses primarily on the statistical analysis of economic and financial time series [2]. The other field is Mathematical Finance [3, 4]. This term implies that finance has given a rise to several new mathematical theories. The leading directions in Mathematical Finance include portfolio theory, option-pricing theory, and risk measurement.

The "academic" part of this book demonstrates that financial data can be an area of exciting theoretical research, which might be of interest to physicists regardless of their career motivation. This part includes the Econophysics topics and the agent-based modeling of financial markets.[1] Physicists use the term Econophysics to emphasize the concepts of theoretical physics (e.g., scaling, fractals, and chaos) that are applied to the analysis of economic and financial data. This field was formed in the early 1990s, and it has been growing rapidly ever since. Several books on Econophysics have been published to date [5–11] as well as numerous articles in the scientific periodical journals such as *Physica A* and *Quantitative Finance*.[2] The agent-based modeling of financial markets was introduced by mathematically inclined economists (see [12] for a review). Not surprisingly, physicists, being accustomed to the modeling of "anything," have contributed into this field, too [7, 10].

Although physicists are the primary audience for this book, two other reader groups may also benefit from it. The first group includes computer science and mathematics majors who are willing to work (or have recently started a career) in the finance industry. In addition, this book may be of interest to majors in economics and finance who are curious about Econophysics and agent-based modeling of financial markets. This book can be used for self-education or in an elective course on Quantitative Finance for science and engineering majors.

The book is organized as follows. Chapter 2 describes the basics of financial markets. Its topics include market price formation, returns and dividends, and market efficiency. The next five chapters outline the theoretical framework of Quantitative Finance: elements of mathematical statistics (Chapter 3), stochastic processes (Chapter 4), time series analysis (Chapter 5), fractals (Chapter 6), and nonlinear dynamical systems (Chapter 7). Although all of these subjects have been exhaustively covered in many excellent sources, we offer this material for self-contained presentation.

In Chapter 3, the basic notions of mathematical statistics are introduced and several popular probability distributions are listed. In particular, the stable distributions that are used in analysis of financial time series are discussed.

Chapter 4 begins with an introduction to the Wiener process, which is the basis for description of the stochastic financial processes. Three methodological approaches are outlined: one is rooted in the generic Markov process, the second one is based on the Langevin equation, and the last one stems from the discrete random walk. Then the basics of stochastic calculus are described. They include the Ito's lemma and the stochastic integral in both the Ito and the Stratonovich forms. Finally, the notion of martingale is introduced.

Chapter 5 begins with the univariate autoregressive and moving average models, the classical tools of the time series analysis. Then the approaches to accounting for trends and seasonality effects are discussed. Furthermore, processes with non-stationary variance (conditional heteroskedasticity) are described. Finally, the specifics of the multivariate time series are outlined.

In Chapter 6, the basic definitions of the fractal theory are discussed. The concept of multifractals, which has been receiving a lot of attention in recent financial time series research, is also introduced.

Chapter 7 describes the elements of nonlinear dynamics that are important for agent-based modeling of financial markets. To illustrate the major concepts in this field, two classical models are discussed: the discrete logistic map and the continuous Lorenz model. The main pathways to chaos and the chaos measures are also outlined.

Those readers who do not need to refresh their knowledge of the mathematical concepts may skip Chapters 3 through 7.[3]

The other five chapters are devoted to financial applications. In Chapter 8, the scaling properties of the financial time series are discussed. The main subject here is the power laws manifesting in the distributions of returns. Alternative approaches in describing the scaling properties of the financial time series including the multifractal models are also outlined.

The next three chapters, Chapters 9 through 11, relate specifically to Mathematical Finance. Chapter 9 is devoted to the option pricing. It starts with the general properties of stock options, and then the option pricing theory is discussed using two approaches: the method of the binomial trees and the classical Black-Scholes theory.

Chapter 10 is devoted to the portfolio theory. Its basics include the capital asset pricing model and the arbitrage pricing theory. Finally, several arbitrage trading strategies are listed. Risk measurement is the subject of Chapter 11. It starts with the concept of value at risk, which is widely used in risk management. Then the notion of coherent risk measure is introduced and one such popular measure, the expected tail losses, is described.

Finally, Chapter 12 is devoted to agent-based modeling of financial markets. Two elaborate models that illustrate two different approaches to defining the price dynamics are described. The first one is based on the supply-demand equilibrium, and the other approach employs an empirical relation between price change and excess demand. Discussion of the model derived in terms of observable variables concludes this chapter.

The bibliography provides the reader with references for further reading rather than with a comprehensive chronological review. The reference list is generally confined with recent monographs and reviews. However, some original work that either has particularly influenced the author or seems to expand the field in promising ways is also included.

In every chapter, exercises with varying complexity are provided. Some of these exercises simply help the readers to get their hands on the financial market data available on the Internet and to manipulate the data using Microsoft Excel software.[4] Other exercises provide a means of testing the understanding of the book's theoretical material. More challenging exercises, which may require consulting with advanced textbooks or implementation of complicated algorithms, are denoted with an asterisk. The exercises denoted with two asterisks offer discussions of recent research reports. The latter exercises may be used for seminar presentations or for course work.

A few words about notations. Scalar values are denoted with the regular font (e.g., X) while vectors and matrices are denoted with boldface letters (e.g., $\mathbf{X}$). The matrix transposes are denoted with primes (e.g., $\mathbf{X}'$) and the matrix determinants are denoted with vertical bars (e.g., $|\mathbf{X}|$). The following notations are used interchangeably: $X(t_k) \equiv X(t)$ and $X(t_{k-1}) \equiv X(t-1)$. $E[X]$ is used to denote the expectation of the variable X.

The views expressed in this book may not reflect the views of my former and current employers. While conducting the Econophysics research and writing this book, I enjoyed support from Blake LeBaron, Thomas Lux, Sorin Solomon, and Eugene Stanley. I am also indebted to anonymous reviewers for attentive analysis of the book's drafts. Needless to say, I am solely responsible for all possible errors present in this edition. I will greatly appreciate all comments about this book; please send them to *a_b_schmidt@hotmail.com.*

Alec Schmidt
Cedar Knolls, NJ, June 2004

Chapter 2

Financial Markets

This chapter begins with a description of market price formation. The notion of return that is widely used for analysis of the investment efficiency is introduced in Section 2.2. Then the dividend effects on return and the present-value pricing model are described. The next big topic is market efficiency (Section 2.3). First, the notion of arbitrage is defined. Then the Efficient Market Hypothesis, both the theory and its critique, are discussed. The pathways for further reading in Section 2.4 conclude the chapter.

2.1 MARKET PRICE FORMATION

Millions of different financial assets (stocks, bonds, currencies, options, and others) are traded around the world. Some financial markets are organized in exchanges or bourses (e.g., New York Stock Exchange (NYSE)). In other, so-called over-the-counter (OTC) markets, participants operate directly via telecommunication systems. Market data are collected and distributed by markets themselves and by financial data services such as Bloomberg and Reuters. Modern electronic networks facilitate access to huge volumes of market data in real time.

Market prices are formed with the trader orders (quotes) submitted on the bid (buy) and ask (sell) sides of the market. Usually, there is a spread between the best (highest) bid and the best (lowest) ask prices, which provides profits for the market makers. The prices seen on the tickers of TV networks and on the Internet are usually the transaction prices that correspond to the best prices. The very presence of trans-actions implies that some traders submit *market orders*; they buy at current best ask prices and sell at current best bid prices. The trans-action prices represent the mere tip of an iceberg beneath which prices of the *limit orders* reside. Indeed, traders may submit the sell orders at prices higher than the best bid and the buy orders at prices lower than the best ask. The limit orders reflect the trader expectations of future price movement. There are also *stop orders* designated to limit pos-sible losses. For an asset holder, the stop order implies selling assets if the price falls to a predetermined value.

Holding assets, particularly holding derivatives (see Section 9.1), is called *long position*. The opposite of long buying is *short selling*, which means selling assets that the trader does not own after borrowing them from the broker. Short selling makes sense if the price is expected to fall. When the price does drop, the short seller buys the same number of assets that were borrowed and returns them to the broker. Short sellers may also use stop orders to limit their losses in case the price grows rather than falls. Namely, they may submit the stop order for triggering a buy when the price reaches a predeter-mined value.

Limit orders and stop orders form the *market microstructure*: the volume-price distributions on the bid and ask sides of the market. The concept *market liquidity* is used to describe price sensitivity to market orders. For instance, low liquidity means that the number of securities available at the best price is smaller than a typical market order. In this case, a new market order is executed within a range of available prices rather than at a single best price. As a result, the best price changes its value. Securities with very low liquidity may have no transactions and few (if any) quotes for some time (in particular, the small-cap stocks off regular trading hours). Market microstructure information usually is not publicly available. However, the market microstructure may be partly revealed in the price reaction to big block trades.

Any event that affects the market microstructure (such as submis-sion, execution, or withdrawal of an order) is called a *tick*. Ticks are recorded along with the time they are submitted (so-called *tick-by-tick data*). Generally, tick-by-tick data are not regularly spaced in time, which leads to additional challenges for high-frequency data analysis [1, 2]. Current research of financial data is overwhelmingly conducted on the homogeneous grids that are defined with filtering and averaging tick-by-tick data.

Another problem that complicates analysis of long financial time series is seasonal patterns. Business hours, holidays, and even daylight saving time shifts affect market activity. Introducing the dummy variables into time series models is a general method to account for seasonal effects (see Section 5.2). In another approach, "operational time" is employed to describe the non-homogeneity of business activity [2]. Non-trading hours, including weekends and holidays, may be cut off from operational time grids.

2.2 RETURNS AND DIVIDENDS

2.2.1 SIMPLE AND COMPOUNDED RETURNS

While price P is the major financial variable, its logarithm, $p = \log(P)$ is often used in quantitative analysis. The primary reason for using log prices is that simulation of a random price innovation can move price into the negative region, which does not make sense. In the mean time, negative logarithm of price is perfectly acceptable.

Another important financial variable is the single-period return (or *simple return*) R(t) that defines the return between two subsequent moments t and t−1. If no dividends are paid,

$$R(t) = P(t)/P(t - 1) - 1 \tag{2.2.1}$$

Return is used as a measure of investment efficiency.[1] Its advantage is that some statistical properties, such as stationarity, may be more applicable to returns rather than to prices [3]. The simple return of a portfolio, $R_p(t)$, equals the weighed sum of returns of the portfolio assets

$$R_p(t) = \sum_{i=1}^{N} w_{ip} R_{ip}(t), \quad \sum_{i=1}^{N} w_{ip} = 1, \tag{2.2.2}$$

where R_{ip} and w_{ip} are return and weight of the i-th portfolio asset, respectively; $i = 1, \ldots, N$.

The multi-period returns, or the *compounded returns,* define the returns between the moments t and $t - k + 1$. The compounded return equals

$$R(t, k) = [R(t) + 1] [R(t - 1) + 1]\dots[R(t - k + 1) + 1] + 1$$
$$= P(t)/P(t - k) + 1 \qquad (2.2.3)$$

The return averaged over k periods equals

$$\check{R}(t, k) = \left[\prod_{i=0}^{k-1} (R(t - i) + 1)\right]^{1/k} - 1 \qquad (2.2.4)$$

If the simple returns are small, the right-hand side of (2.2.4) can be reduced to the first term of its Taylor expansion:

$$\check{R}(t, k) \approx \frac{1}{k}\sum_{i=1}^{k-1} R(t, i) \qquad (2.2.5)$$

The *continuously compounded return* (or *log return*) is defined as:

$$r(t) = \log[R(t) + 1] = p(t) - p(t - 1) \qquad (2.2.6)$$

Calculation of the compounded log returns is reduced to simple summation:

$$r(t, k) = r(t) + r(t - 1) + \dots + r(t - k + 1) \qquad (2.2.7)$$

However, the weighing rule (2.2.2) is not applicable to the log returns since log of sum is not equal to sum of logs.

2.2.2 DIVIDEND EFFECTS

If dividends $D(t + 1)$ are paid within the period $[t, t + 1]$, the simple return (see 2.2.1) is modified to

$$R(t + 1) = [P(t + 1) + D(t + 1)]/P(t) - 1 \qquad (2.2.8)$$

The compounded returns and the log returns are calculated in the same way as in the case with no dividends.

Dividends play a critical role in the *discounted-cash-flow* (or *present-value*) *pricing model*. Before describing this model, let us introduce the notion of *present value*. Consider the amount of cash K invested in a risk-free asset with the interest rate r. If interest is paid every time interval (say every month), the *future value* of this cash after n periods is equal to

$$FV = K(1 + r)^n \qquad (2.2.9)$$

Suppose we are interested in finding out what amount of money will yield given *future value* after n intervals. This amount (present value) equals

$$PV = FV/(1 + r)^n \qquad (2.2.10)$$

Calculating the present value via the future value is called *discounting*. The notions of the present value and the future value determine the payoff of so-called zero-coupon bonds. These bonds sold at their present value promise a single payment of their future value at maturity date.

The discounted-cash-flow model determines the stock price via its future cash flow. For the simple model with the constant return $E[R(t)] = R$, one can rewrite (2.2.8) as

$$P(t) = E[\{P(t + 1) + D(t + 1)\}/(1 + R)] \qquad (2.2.11)$$

If this recursion is repeated K times, one obtains

$$P(t) = E\left[\sum_{i=1}^{K} D(t + i)/(1 + R)^i\right] + E[P(t + K)/(1 + R)^K] \qquad (2.2.12)$$

In the limit $K \to \infty$, the second term in the right-hand side of (2.2.12) can be neglected if

$$\lim_{K \to \infty} E[P(t + K)/(1 + R)^K] = 0 \qquad (2.2.13)$$

Then the discounted-cash-flow model yields

$$P_D(t) = E\left[\sum_{i=1}^{\infty} D(t + i)/(1 + R)^i\right] \qquad (2.2.14)$$

Further simplification of the discounted-cash-flow model is based on the assumption that the dividends grow linearly with rate G

$$E[D(t + i)] = (1 + G)^i D(t) \qquad (2.2.15)$$

Then (2.2.14) reduces to

$$P_D(t) = \frac{1+G}{R-G} D(t) \qquad (2.2.16)$$

Obviously, equation (2.2.16) makes sense only for $R > G$. The value of R that may attract investors is called the *required rate of return*. This value can be treated as the sum of the risk-free rate and the asset risk premium. While the assumption of linear dividend growth is unrealistic, equation (2.2.16) shows the high sensitivity of price to change in the discount rate R when R is close to G (see Exercise 2). A detailed analysis of the discounted-cash-flow model is given in [3].

   If the condition (2.2.13) does not hold, the solution to (2.2.12) can be presented in the form

$$P(t) = P_D(t) + B(t), \quad B(t) = E[B(t+1)/(1+R)] \qquad (2.2.17)$$

The term $P_D(t)$ has the sense of the fundamental value while the function $B(t)$ is often called the *rational bubble*. This term implies that $B(t)$ may lead to unbounded growth—the "bubble." Yet, this bubble is "rational" since it is based on rational expectations of future returns. In the popular Blanchard-Watson model

$$B(t+1) = \begin{cases} \dfrac{1+R}{\pi} B(t) + \varepsilon(t+1) \text{ with probability } \pi, 0 < \pi < 1 \\ \varepsilon(t+1) \text{ with probability } 1 - \pi \end{cases} \qquad (2.2.18)$$

where $\varepsilon(t)$ is an *independent and identically distributed process (IID)*[2] with $E[\varepsilon(t)] = 0$. The specific of this model is that it describes periodically collapsing bubbles (see [4] for the recent research).

   So far, the discrete presentation of financial data was discussed. Clearly, market events have a discrete nature and price variations cannot be smaller than certain values. Yet, the continuum presentation of financial processes is often employed [5]. This means that the time interval between two consecutive market events compared to the time range of interest is so small that it can be considered an infinitesimal difference. Often, the price discreteness can also be neglected since the markets allow for quoting prices with very small differentials. The future value and the present value within the continuous presentation equal, respectively

$$FV = K \exp(rt), \quad PV = FV \exp(-rt) \qquad (2.2.19)$$

In the following chapters, both the discrete and the continuous presentations will be used.

2.3 MARKET EFFICIENCY

2.3.1 ARBITRAGE

Asset prices generally obey the Law of One Price, which says that prices of equivalent assets in competitive markets must be the same [6]. This implies that if a security replicates a package of other securities, the price of this security and the price of the package it replicates must be equal. It is expected also that the asset price must be the same worldwide, provided that it is expressed in the same currency and that the transportation and transaction costs can be neglected. Violation of the Law of One Price leads to *arbitrage*, which means buying an asset and immediate selling it (usually in another market) with profit and without risk. One widely publicized example of arbitrage is the notable differences in prices of prescription drugs in the USA, Europe, and Canada. Another typical example is the so-called triangle foreign exchange arbitrage. Consider a situation in which a trader can exchange one American dollar (USD) for one Euro (EUR) or for 120 Yen (JPY). In addition, a trader can exchange one EUR for 119 JPY. Hence, in terms of the exchange rates, 1 USD/JPY > 1 EUR/JPY * 1 USD/EUR.[3] Obviously, the trader who operates, say 100000 USD, can make a profit by buying 12000000 JPY, then selling them for 12000000/119 ≈ 100840 EUR, and then buying back 100840 USD. If the transaction costs are neglected, this operation will bring profit of about 840 USD.

The arbitrage with prescription drugs persists due to unresolved legal problems. However, generally the arbitrage opportunities do not exist for long. The triangle arbitrage may appear from time to time. Foreign exchange traders make a living, in part, by finding such opportunities. They rush to exchange USD for JPY. It is important to remember that, as it was noted in Section 2.1, there is only a finite number of assets at the "best" price. In our example, it is a finite number of Yens available at the exchange rate USD/JPY = 120. As soon as they all are taken, the exchange rate USD/JPY falls to the equilibrium value 1 USD/JPY = 1 EUR/JPY * 1 USD/EUR, and the arbitrage vanishes. In general, when arbitrageurs take profits, they act in a way that eliminates arbitrage opportunities.

2.3.2 EFFICIENT MARKET HYPOTHESIS (EMH)

Efficient market is closely related to (the absence of) arbitrage. It might be defined as simply an ideal market without arbitrage, but there is much more to it than that. Let us first ask what actually causes price to change. The share price of a company may change due to its new earnings report, due to new prognosis of the company performance, or due to a new outlook for the industry trend. Macroeconomic and political events, or simply gossip about a company's management, can also affect the stock price. All these events imply that new information becomes available to markets. The *Efficient Market Theory* states that financial markets are efficient because they instantly reflect all new relevant information in asset prices. *Efficient Market Hypothesis* (EMH) proposes the way to evaluate market efficiency. For example, an investor in an efficient market should not expect earnings above the market return while using *technical analysis* or *fundamental analysis*.[4]

Three forms of EMH are discerned in modern economic literature. In the "weak" form of EMH, current prices reflect all information on past prices. Then the technical analysis seems to be helpless. In the "strong" form, prices instantly reflect not only public but also private (insider) information. This implies that the fundamental analysis (which is what the investment analysts do) is not useful either. The compromise between the strong and weak forms yields the "semi-strong" form of EMH according to which prices reflect all publicly available information and the investment analysts play important role in defining *fair prices*.

Two notions are important for EMH. The first notion is *the random walk*, which will be formally defined in Section 5.1. In short, market prices follow the random walk if their variations are random and independent. Another notion is *rational investors* who immediately incorporate new information into fair prices. The evolution of the EMH paradigm, starting with Bachelier's pioneering work on random price behavior back in 1900 to the formal definition of EMH by Fama in 1965 to the rigorous statistical analysis by Lo and MacKinlay in the late 1980s, is well publicized [9–13]. If prices follow the random walk, this is the sufficient condition for EMH. However, as we shall discuss further, the pragmatic notion of market efficiency does not necessarily require prices to follow the random walk.

Criticism of EMH has been conducted along two avenues. First, the thorough theoretical analysis has resulted in rejection of the random walk hypothesis for the weekly U.S. market returns during 1962–1986 [12]. Interestingly, similar analysis for the period of 1986–1996 shows that the returns conform more closely to the random walk. As the authors of this research, Lo and MacKinlay, suggest, one possible reason for this trend is that several investment firms had implemented *statistical arbitrage* trading strategies[5] based on the market inefficiencies that were revealed in early research. Execution of these strategies could possibly eliminate some of the arbitrage opportunities.

Another reason for questioning EMH is that the notions of "fair price" and "rational investors" do not stand criticism in the light of the financial market booms and crashes. The "irrational exuberance" in 1999–2000 can hardly be attributed to rational behavior [10]. In fact, empirical research in the new field "behavioral finance" demonstrates that investor behavior often differs from rationality [14, 15]. Overconfidence, indecisiveness, overreaction, and a willingness to gamble are among the psychological traits that do not fit rational behavior. A widely popularized example of irrational human behavior was described by Kahneman and Tversky [16]. While conducting experiments with volunteers, they asked participants to make choices in two different situations. First, participants with $1000 were given a choice between: (a) gambling with a 50% chance of gaining $1000 and a 50% chance of gaining nothing, or (b) a sure gain of $500. In the second situation, participants with $2000 were given a choice between: (a) a 50% chance of losing $1000 and a 50% of losing nothing, and (b) a sure loss of $500. Thus, the option (b) in both situations guaranteed a gain of $1500. Yet, the majority of participants chose option (b) in the first situation and option (a) in the second one. Hence, participants preferred sure yet smaller gains but were willing to gamble in order to avoid sure loss.

Perhaps Keynes' explanation that "animal spirits" govern investor behavior is an exaggeration. Yet investors cannot be reduced to completely rational machines either. Moreover, actions of different investors, while seemingly rational, may significantly vary. In part, this may be caused by different perceptions of market events and trends (heterogeneous beliefs). In addition, investors may have different resources for acquiring and processing new information. As a result, the notion of so-called *bounded rationality* has become popular in modern economic literature (see also Section 12.2).

Still the advocates of EMH do not give up. Malkiel offers the following argument in the section "What do we mean by saying markets are efficient" of his book "A Random Walk down Wall Street" [9]:

> "No one person or institution has yet to provide a long-term, consistent record of finding risk-adjusted individual stock trading opportunities, particularly if they pay taxes and incur transactions costs."

Thus, polemics on EMH changes the discussion from whether prices follow the random walk to the practical ability to consistently "beat the market."

Whatever experts say, the search of ideas yielding excess returns never ends. In terms of the quantification level, three main directions in the investment strategies may be discerned. First, there are qualitative receipts such as "Dogs of the Dow" (buying 10 stocks of the Dow Jones Industrial Average with highest dividend yield), "January Effect" (stock returns are particularly high during the first two January weeks), and others. These ideas are arguably not a reliable profit source [9].

Then there are relatively simple patterns of technical analysis, such as "channel," "head and shoulders," and so on (see, e.g., [7]). There has been ongoing academic discussion on whether technical analysis is able to yield persistent excess returns (see, e.g., [17–19] and references therein). Finally, there are trading strategies based on sophisticated statistical arbitrage. While several trading firms that employ these strategies have proven to be profitable in some periods, little is known about persistent efficiency of their proprietary strategies. Recent trends indicate that some statistical arbitrage opportunities may be fading [20]. Nevertheless, one may expect that modern, extremely volatile markets will always provide new occasions for aggressive arbitrageurs.

2.4 PATHWAYS FOR FURTHER READING

In this chapter, a few abstract statistical notions such as IID and random walk were mentioned. In the next five chapters, we take a short tour of the mathematical concepts that are needed for acquaintance with quantitative finance. Those readers who feel confident in their mathematical background may jump ahead to Chapter 8.

Regarding further reading for this chapter, general introduction to finance can be found in [6]. The history of development and validation of EMH is described in several popular books [9–11].[6] On the MBA level, much of the material pertinent to this chapter is given in [3].

EXERCISES

1. Familiarize yourself with the financial market data available on the Internet (e.g., *http://www.finance.yahoo.com*). Download the weekly closing prices of the exchange-traded fund SPDR that replicates the S&P 500 index (ticker SPY) for 1996–2003. Calculate simple weekly returns for this data sample (we shall use these data for other exercises).

2. Calculate the present value of SPY for 2004 if the asset risk premium is equal to (a) 3% and (b) 4%. The SPY dividends in 2003 were $1.63. Assume the dividend growth rate of 5% (see Exercise 5.3 for a more accurate estimate). Assume the risk-free rate of 3%. What risk premium was priced in SPY in the end of 2004 according to the discounted-cash-flow theory?

3. Simulate the rational bubble using the Blanchard-Watson model (2.2.18). Define $\varepsilon(t) = P_U(t) - 0.5$ where P_U is standard uniform distribution (explain why the relation $\varepsilon(t) = P_U(t)$ cannot be used). Use $\pi = 0.75$ and $R = 0.1$ as the initial values for studying the model sensitivity to the input parameters.

4. Is there an arbitrage opportunity for the following set of the exchange rates: GBP/USD = 1.7705, EUR/USD = 1.1914, EUR/GBP = 0.6694?

Chapter 3

Probability Distributions

This chapter begins with the basic notions of mathematical statistics that form the framework for analysis of financial data (see, e.g., [1–3]). In Section 3.2, a number of distributions widely used in statistical data analysis are listed. The stable distributions that have become popular in Econophysics research are discussed in Section 3.3.

3.1 BASIC DEFINITIONS

Consider the random variable (or *variate*) X. The *probability density function* P(x) defines the probability to find X between a and b

$$\Pr(a \leq X \leq b) = \int_a^b P(x)dx \tag{3.1.1}$$

The probability density must be a non-negative function and must satisfy the normalization condition

$$\int_{X_{min}}^{X_{max}} P(x)dx = 1 \tag{3.1.2}$$

where the interval $[X_{min}, X_{max}]$ is the range of all possible values of X. In fact, the infinite limits $[-\infty, \infty]$ can always be used since P(x) may be set to zero outside the interval [X_{min}, X_{max}]. As a rule, the infinite integration limits are further omitted.

Another way of describing random variable is to use the *cumulative distribution function*

$$Pr(X \leq b) = \int_{-\infty}^{b} P(x)dx \qquad (3.1.3)$$

Obviously, probability satisfies the condition

$$Pr(X > b) = 1 - Pr(X \leq b) \qquad (3.1.4)$$

Two characteristics are used to describe probable values of random variable X: *mean* (or *expectation*) and *median*. Mean of X is the average of all possible values of X that are weighed with the probability density P(x)

$$m \equiv E[X] = \int xP(x)dx \qquad (3.1.5)$$

Median of X is the value, M, for which

$$Pr(X > M) = Pr(X < M) = 0.5 \qquad (3.1.6)$$

Median is the preferable characteristic of the most probable value for strongly skewed data samples. Consider a sample of lottery tickets that has one "lucky" ticket winning one million dollars and 999 "losers." The mean win in this sample is $1000, which does not realistically describe the lottery outcome. The median zero value is a much more relevant characteristic in this case.

The expectation of a random variable calculated using some available information I_t (that may change with time t) is called *conditional expectation*. The conditional probability density is denoted by $P(x|I_t)$. Conditional expectation equals

$$E[X_t|I_t] = \int xP(x|I_t)dx \qquad (3.1.7)$$

Variance, Var, and the *standard deviation*, σ, are the conventional estimates of the deviations from the mean values of X

$$Var[X] \equiv \sigma^2 = \int (x - m)^2 P(x)dx \qquad (3.1.8)$$

In financial literature, the standard deviation of price is used to characterize the price *volatility*.

The higher-order moments of the probability distributions are defined as

$$m_n \equiv E[X^n] = \int x^n P(x) dx \qquad (3.1.9)$$

According to this definition, mean is the first moment ($m \equiv m_1$), and variance can be expressed via the first two moments, $\sigma^2 = m_2 - m^2$. Two other important parameters, *skewness* S and *kurtosis* K, are related to the third and fourth moments, respectively,

$$S = E[(x - m)^3]/\sigma^3, \ K = E[(x - m)^4]/\sigma^4 \qquad (3.1.10)$$

Both parameters, S and K, are dimensionless. Zero skewness implies that the distribution is symmetrical around its mean value. The positive and negative values of skewness indicate long positive tails and long negative tails, respectively. Kurtosis characterizes the distribution peakedness. Kurtosis of the normal distribution equals three. The excess kurtosis, $K_e = K - 3$, is often used as a measure of deviation from the normal distribution. In particular, positive excess kurtosis (or *leptokurtosis*) indicates more frequent medium and large deviations from the mean value than is typical for the normal distribution. Leptokurtosis leads to a flatter central part and to so-called fat tails in the distribution. Negative excess kurtosis indicates frequent small deviations from the mean value. In this case, the distribution sharpens around its mean value while the distribution tails decay faster than the tails of the normal distribution.

The *joint distribution* of two random variables X and Y is the generalization of the cumulative distribution (see 3.1.3)

$$Pr(X \leq b, Y \leq c) = \int_{-\infty}^{b} \int_{-\infty}^{c} h(x, y) dx dy \qquad (3.1.11)$$

In (3.1.11), h(x, y) is the joint density that satisfies the normalization condition

$$\int_{-\infty}^{\infty} \int_{-\infty}^{\infty} h(x, y) dx dy = 1 \qquad (3.1.12)$$

Two random variables are *independent* if their joint density function is simply the product of the univariate density functions: $h(x, y) = f(x)g(y)$. *Covariance* between two variates provides a measure of their simultaneous change. Consider two variates, X and Y, that have the means m_X and m_Y, respectively. Their covariance equals

$$\text{Cov}(x, y) \equiv \sigma_{XY} = E[(x - m_X)(y - m_Y)] = E[xy] - m_X m_Y \quad (3.1.13)$$

Obviously, covariance reduces to variance if $X = Y$: $\sigma_{XX} = \sigma_X^2$. Positive covariance between two variates implies that these variates tend to change simultaneously in the same direction rather than in opposite directions. Conversely, negative covariance between two variates implies that when one variate grows, the second one tends to fall and vice versa. Another popular measure of simultaneous change is the *correlation coefficient*

$$\text{Corr}(x, y) = \text{Cov}(x.y)/(\sigma_X \, \sigma_Y) \quad (3.1.14)$$

The values of the correlation coefficient are within the range $[-1, 1]$. In the general case with N variates $X_1, \ldots, X_N$ (where $N > 2$), correlations among variates are described with *the covariance matrix*. Its elements equal

$$\text{Cov}(x_i, x_j) \equiv \sigma_{ij} = E[(x_i - m_i)(x_j - m_j)] \quad (3.1.15)$$

3.2 IMPORTANT DISTRIBUTIONS

There are several important probability distributions used in quantitative finance. The *uniform distribution* has a constant value within the given interval [a, b] and equals zero outside this interval

$$P_U = \begin{cases} 0, \, x < a \text{ and } x > b \\ 1/(b - a), \, a \leq x \leq b \end{cases} \quad (3.2.1)$$

The uniform distribution has the following mean and higher-order moments

$$m_U = 0, \, \sigma^2_U = (b - a)^2/12, \, S_U = 0, \, K_{eU} = -6/5 \quad (3.2.2)$$

The case with $a = 0$ and $b = 1$ is called the *standard uniform distribution*. Many computer languages and software packages have a library function for calculating the standard uniform distribution.

The *binomial distribution* is a discrete distribution of obtaining n successes out of N trials where the result of each trial is true with probability p and is false with probability $q = 1 - p$ (so-called *Bernoulli trials*)

$$P_B(n; N, p) = C_{Nn} \, p^n q^{N-n} = C_{Nn} p^n (1 - p)^{N-n}, \; C_{Nn} = \frac{N!}{n!(N - n)!} \quad (3.2.3)$$

The factor C_{Nn} is called the binomial coefficient. Mean and higher-order moments for the binomial distribution are equal, respectively,

$$m_B = Np, \; \sigma^2_B = Np(1 - p), \; S_B = (q - p)/\sigma_B, \; K_{eB} = (1 - 6pq)/\sigma_B^2 \quad (3.2.4)$$

In the case of large N and large $(N - n)$, the binomial distribution approaches the form

$$P_B(n) = \frac{1}{\sqrt{2\pi}\sigma_B} \exp[-(x - m_B)^2/2\sigma^2_B], \; N \to \infty, \; (N - n) \to \infty \quad (3.2.5)$$

that coincides with the *normal* (or *Gaussian*) *distribution* (see 3.2.9). In the case with $p \ll 1$, the binomial distribution approaches the Poisson distribution.

The *Poisson distribution* describes the probability of n successes in N trials assuming that the fraction of successes v is proportional to the number of trials: $v = pN$

$$P_P(n, N) = \frac{N!}{n!(N - n)!} \left(\frac{v}{N}\right)^n \left(1 - \frac{v}{N}\right)^{N-n} \quad (3.2.6)$$

As the number of trials N becomes very large $(N \to \infty)$, equation (3.2.6) approaches the limit

$$P_P(n) = v^n e^{-v}/n! \quad (3.2.7)$$

Mean, variance, skewness, and excess kurtosis of the Poisson distribution are equal, respectively,

$$m_P = \sigma_P^2 = v, \; S_P = v^{-1/2}, \; K_{eP} = v^{-1} \quad (3.2.8)$$

The *normal (Gaussian) distribution* has the form

$$P_N(x) = \frac{1}{\sqrt{2\pi}\sigma} \exp[-(x - m)^2/2\sigma^2] \quad (3.2.9)$$

It is often denoted N(m, σ). Skewness and excess kurtosis of the normal distribution equals zero. The transform $z = (x - m)/\sigma$ converts the normal distribution into the *standard normal distribution*

$$P_{SN}(z) = \frac{1}{\sqrt{2\pi}} \exp[-z^2/2] \qquad (3.2.10)$$

Note that the probability for the standard normal variate to assume the value in the interval [0, z] can be used as the definition of the *error function* erf(x)

$$\frac{1}{\sqrt{2\pi}} \int_0^z \exp(-x^2/2)dx = 0.5 \text{ erf}(z/\sqrt{2}) \qquad (3.2.11)$$

Then the cumulative distribution function for the standard normal distribution equals

$$Pr_{SN}(z) = 0.5[1 + \text{erf}(z/\sqrt{2})] \qquad (3.2.12)$$

According to the *central limit theorem*, the probability density distribution for a sum of N independent random variables with finite variances and finite means approaches the normal distribution as N grows to infinity. Due to exponential decay of the normal distribution, large deviations from its mean rarely appear. The normal distribution plays an extremely important role in all kinds of applications. The Box-Miller method is often used for modeling the normal distribution with given uniform distribution [4]. Namely, if two numbers x_1 and x_2 are drawn from the standard uniform distribution, then y_1 and y_2 are the standard normal variates

$$y_1 = [-2\ln x_1)]^{1/2}\cos(2\pi x_2), \; y_2 = [-2\ln x_1)]^{1/2}\sin(2\pi x_2) \quad (3.2.13)$$

Mean and variance of the multivariate normal distribution with N variates can be easily calculated via the univariate means m_i and covariances σ_{ij}

$$m_N = \sum_{i=1}^{N} m_i, \; \sigma_N^2 = \sum_{i,\,j=1}^{N} \sigma_{ij} \qquad (3.2.14)$$

The *lognormal distribution* is a distribution in which the logarithm of a variate has the normal form

$$P_{LN}(x) = \frac{1}{xs\sqrt{2\pi}} \exp\left[-(\ln\ x - \mu)^2/2s^2\right] \tag{3.2.15}$$

Mean, variance, skewness, and excess kurtosis of the lognormal distribution can be expressed in terms of the parameters s and μ

$$m_{LN} = \exp(\mu + 0.5s^2),$$

$$\sigma_{LN}^2 = [\exp(s^2) - 1]\exp(2\mu + s^2),$$

$$S_{LN} = [\exp(s^2) - 1]^{1/2}[\exp(s^2) + 2],$$

$$K_{eLN} = \exp(4s^2) + 2\exp(3s^2) + 3\exp(2s^2) - 6 \tag{3.2.16}$$

The *Cauchy distribution (Lorentzian)* is an example of the stable distribution (see the next section). It has the form

$$P_C(x) = \frac{b}{\pi[b^2 + (x - m)^2]} \tag{3.2.17}$$

The specific of the Cauchy distribution is that all its moments are infinite. The case with $b = 1$ and $m = 0$ is named *the standard Cauchy distribution*

$$P_C(x) = \frac{1}{\pi[1 + x^2]} \tag{3.2.18}$$

Figure 3.1 depicts the distribution of the weekly returns of the exchange-traded fund SPDR that replicates the S&P 500 index (ticker SPY) for 1996–2003 in comparison with standard normal distribution and the standard Cauchy distributions (see Exercise 3).

The *extreme value distributions* can be introduced with the *Fisher-Tippett theorem*. According to this theorem, if the cumulative distribution function $F(x) = \Pr(X \le x)$ for a random variable X exists, then the cumulative distribution of the maximum values of $X, H_\xi(x) = \Pr(X_{max} \le x)$ has the following asymptotic form

$$H_\xi(x) = \begin{cases} \exp[-(1 + \xi(x - \mu_{max})/\sigma_{max})^{-1/\xi}], & \xi \ne 0, \\ \exp[-\exp(-(x - \mu_{max})/\sigma_{max})], & \xi = 0 \end{cases} \tag{3.2.19}$$

where $1 + \xi(x - \mu_{max})/\sigma_{max} > 0$ in the case with $\xi \ne 0$. In (3.2.19), μ_{max} and σ_{max} are the location and scale parameters, respectively; ξ is the shape parameter and $1/\xi$ is named the tail index. The

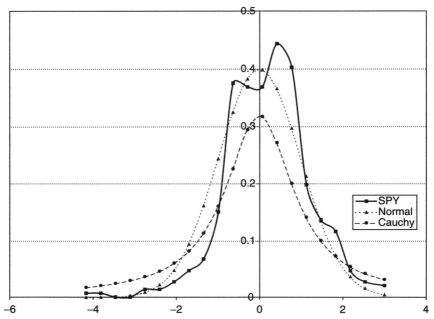

Figure 3.1 The standardized distribution of the weekly returns of the S&P 500 SPDR (SPY) for 1996–2003 in comparison with the standard normal and the standard Cauchy distributions.

Fisher-Tippett theorem does not define the values of the parameters μ_{max} and σ_{max}. However, special methods have been developed for their estimation [5].

It is said that the cumulative distribution function $F(x)$ is in the domain of attraction of $H_\xi(x)$. The tail behavior of the distribution $F(x)$ defines the shape parameter. The *Gumbel distribution* corresponds to the case with $\xi = 0$. Distributions with thin tails, such as normal, lognormal, and exponential distributions, have the Gumbel domain of attraction. The case with $\xi > 0$ is named the *Frechet distribution*. Domain of the Frechet attraction corresponds to distributions with fat tails, such as the Cauchy distribution and the *Pareto distribution* (see the next Section). Finally, the case with $\xi < 0$ defines the *Weibull distribution*. This type of distributions (e.g., the uniform distribution) has a finite tail.

3.3 STABLE DISTRIBUTIONS AND SCALE INVARIANCE

The principal property of *stable distribution* is that the sum of variates has the same distribution shape as that of addends (see, e.g., [6] for details). Both the Cauchy distribution and the normal distribution are stable. This means, in particular, that the sum of two normal distributions with the same mean and variance is also the normal distribution (see Exercise 2). The general definition for the stable distributions was given by Levy. Therefore, the stable distributions are also called the *Levy distributions*.

Consider the Fourier transform $F(q)$ of the probability distribution function $f(x)$

$$F(q) = \int f(x)e^{iqx}dx \qquad (3.3.1)$$

The function $F(q)$ is also called the *characteristic function* of the stochastic process. It can be shown that the logarithm of the characteristic function for the Levy distribution has the following form

$$\ln F_L(q) = \begin{cases} i\mu q - \gamma|q|^{\alpha}[1 - i\beta\delta\tan(\pi\alpha/2)], & \text{if } \alpha \neq 1 \\ i\mu q - \gamma|q|[1 + 2i\beta\delta\ln(|q|)/\pi)], & \text{if } \alpha = 1 \end{cases} \qquad (3.3.2)$$

In (3.3.2), $\delta = q/|q|$ and the distribution parameters must satisfy the following conditions

$$0 < \alpha \leq 2, \ -1 \leq \beta \leq 1, \gamma > 0 \qquad (3.3.3)$$

The parameter μ corresponds to the mean of the stable distribution and can be any real number. The parameter α characterizes the distribution peakedness. If $\alpha = 2$, the distribution is normal. The parameter β characterizes skewness of the distribution. Note that skewness of the normal distribution equals zero and the parameter β does not affect the characteristic function with $\alpha = 2$. For the normal distribution

$$\ln F_N(q) = i\mu q - \gamma q^2 \qquad (3.3.4)$$

The non-negative parameter γ is the scale factor that characterizes the spread of the distribution. In the case of the normal distribution, $\gamma = \sigma^2/2$ (where σ^2 is variance). The Cauchy distribution is defined with the parameters $\alpha = 1$ and $\beta = 0$. Its characteristic function equals

$$\ln F_C(q) = i\mu q - \gamma|q| \tag{3.3.5}$$

The important feature of the stable distributions with $\alpha < 2$ is that they exhibit the power-law decay at large absolute values of the argument x

$$f_L(|x|) \sim |x|^{-(1+\alpha)} \tag{3.3.6}$$

The distributions with the power-law asymptotes are also named the *Pareto distributions*. Many processes exhibit power-law asymptotic behavior. Hence, there has been persistent interest to the stable distributions.

The power-law distributions describe the *scale-free processes*. Scale invariance of a distribution means that it has a similar shape on different scales of independent variables. Namely, function $f(x)$ is scale-invariant to transformation $x \rightarrow \alpha x$ if there is such parameter L that

$$f(x) = Lf(\alpha x) \tag{3.3.7}$$

The solution to equation (3.3.7) is simply the power law

$$f(x) = x^n \tag{3.3.8}$$

where $n = -\ln(L)/\ln(\alpha)$. The power-law function $f(x)$ (3.3.8) is scale-free since the ratio $f(\alpha x)/f(x) = L$ does not depend on x. Note that the parameter α is closely related to the fractal dimension of the function $f(x)$. The fractal theory will be discussed in Chapter 6.

Unfortunately, the moments of stable processes $E[x^n]$ with power-law asymptotes (i.e., when $\alpha < 2$) diverge for $n \geq \alpha$. As a result, the mean of a stable process is infinite when $\alpha \leq 1$. In addition, variance of a stable process is infinite when $\alpha < 2$. Therefore, the normal distribution is the only stable distribution with finite mean and finite variance.

The stable distributions have very helpful features for data analysis such as flexible description of peakedness and skewness. However, as it was mentioned previously, the usage of the stable distributions in financial applications is often restricted because of their infinite variance at $\alpha < 2$. The compromise that retains flexibility of the Levy distribution yet yields finite variance is named *truncated Levy flight*. This distribution is defined as [2]

$$f_{TL}(x) = \begin{cases} 0, & |x| > \ell \\ Cf_L(x), & -\ell \leq x \leq \ell \end{cases} \tag{3.3.9}$$

In (3.3.9), $f_L(x)$ is the Levy distribution ℓ is the cutoff length, and C is the normalization constant. Sometimes the exponential cut-off is used at large distances [3]

$$f_{TL}(x) \sim \exp(-\lambda|x|), \lambda > 0, |x| > \ell \tag{3.3.10}$$

Since $f_{TL}(x)$ has finite variance, it converges to the normal distribution according to the central limit theorem.

3.4 REFERENCES FOR FURTHER READING

The Feller's textbook is the classical reference to the probability theory [1]. The concept of scaling in financial data has been advocated by Mandelbrot since the 1960s (see the collection of his work in [7]). This problem is widely discussed in the current Econophysics literature [2, 3, 8].

3.5 EXERCISES

1. Calculate the correlation coefficients between the prices of Microsoft (MSFT), Intel (INTC), and Wal-Mart (WMT). Use monthly closing prices for the period 1994–2003. What do you think of the opposite signs for some of these coefficients?
2. Familiarize yourself with Microsoft Excel's statistical tools. Assuming that Z is the standard normal distribution: (a) calculate $Pr(1 \leq Z \leq 3)$ using the NORMSDIST function; (b) calculate x such that $Pr(Z \leq x) = 0.95$ using the NORMSINV function; (c) calculate x such that $Pr(Z \geq x) = 0.15$; (d) generate 100 random numbers from the standard normal distribution using Tools/ Data Analysis/Random Number Generation. Calculate the sample mean and standard variance. How do they differ from the theoretical values of m = 0 and $\sigma = 1$, respectively? (e) Do the same for the standard uniform distribution as in (d).

(f) Generate 100 normally distributed random numbers x using the function x = NORMSINV(z) where z is taken from a sample of the standard uniform distribution. Explain why it is possible. Calculate the sample mean and the standard deviation. How do they differ from the theoretical values of m and σ, respectively?

3. Calculate mean, standard deviation, excess kurtosis, and skew for the SPY data sample from Exercise 2.1. Draw the distribution function of this data set in comparison with the standard normal distribution and the standard Cauchy distribution. Compare results with Figure 3.1.

   Hint: (1) Normalize returns by subtracting their mean and dividing the results by the standard deviation. (2) Calculate the histogram using the Histogram tool of the Data Analysis menu. (3) Divide the histogram frequencies with the product of their sum and the bin size (explain why it is necessary).

4. Let X_1 and X_2 be two independent copies of the normal distribution $X \sim N(\mu, \sigma^2)$. Since X is stable, $aX_1 + bX_2 \sim CX + D$. Calculate C and D via given μ, σ, a, and b.

Chapter 4

Stochastic Processes

Financial variables, such as prices and returns, are random time-dependent variables. The notion of *stochastic process* is used to describe their behavior. Specifically, the Wiener process (or the Brownian motion) plays the central role in mathematical finance. Section 4.1 begins with the generic path: Markov process $\rightarrow$ Chapmen-Kolmogorov equation $\rightarrow$ Fokker-Planck equation $\rightarrow$ Wiener process. This methodology is supplemented with two other approaches in Section 4.2. Namely, the Brownian motion is derived using the Langevin's equation and the discrete random walk. Then the basics of stochastic calculus are described. In particular, the stochastic differential equation is defined using the Ito's lemma (Section 4.3), and the stochastic integral is given in both the Ito and the Stratonovich forms (Section 4.4). Finally, the notion of martingale, which is widely popular in mathematical finance, is introduced in Section 4.5.

4.1 MARKOV PROCESSES

Consider a process $X(t)$ for which the values x_1, x_2, ... are measured at times t_1, t_2, ... Here, one-dimensional variable x is used for notational simplicity, though extension to multidimensional systems is trivial. It is assumed that the joint probability density $f(x_1, t_1; x_2, t_2; ...)$ exists and defines the system completely. The conditional probability density function is defined as

$$f(x_1, t_1; x_2, t_2; \ldots x_k, t_k | x_{k+1}, t_{k+1}; x_{k+2}, t_{k+2}; \ldots) =$$
$$f(x_1, t_1; x_2, t_2; \ldots x_{k+1}, t_{k+1}; \ldots)/f(x_{k+1}, t_{k+1}; x_{k+2}, t_{k+2}; \ldots) \quad (4.1.1)$$

In (4.1.1) and further in this section, $t_1 > t_2 > \ldots t_k > t_{k+1} > \ldots$ unless stated otherwise. In the simplest stochastic process, the present has no dependence on the past. The probability density function for such a process equals

$$f(x_1, t_1; x_2, t_2; \ldots) = f(x_1, t_1)f(x_2, t_2) \ldots \equiv \prod_i f(x_i, t_i) \quad (4.1.2)$$

The *Markov process* represents the next level of complexity, which embraces an extremely wide class of phenomena. In this process, the future depends on the present but not on the past. Hence, its conditional probability density function equals

$$f(x_1, t_1; x_2, t_2; \ldots x_k, t_k | x_{k+1}, t_{k+1}; x_{k+2}, t_{k+2}; \ldots) =$$
$$f(x_1, t_1; x_2, t_2; \ldots x_k, t_k | x_{k+1}, t_{k+1}) \quad (4.1.3)$$

This means that evolution of the system is determined with the *initial condition* (i.e., with the value x_{k+1} at time t_{k+1}). It follows for the Markov process that

$$f(x_1, t_1; x_2, t_2; x_3, t_3) = f(x_1, t_1 | x_2, t_2)f(x_2, t_2 | x_3, t_3) \quad (4.1.4)$$

Using the definition of the conditional probability density, one can introduce the general equation

$$f(x_1, t_1 | x_3, t_3) = \int f(x_1, t_1; x_2, t_2 | x_3, t_3)dx_2$$
$$= \int f(x_1, t_1 | x_2, t_2; x_3, t_3)f(x_2, t_2 | x_3, t_3)dx_2 \quad (4.1.5)$$

For the Markov process,

$$f(x_1, t_1 | x_2, t_2; x_3, t_3) = f(x_1, t_1 | x_2, t_2), \quad (4.1.6)$$

Then the substitution of equation (4.1.6) into equation (4.1.5) leads to the *Chapmen-Kolmogorov equation*

$$f(x_1, t_1 | x_3, t_3) = \int f(x_1, t_1 | x_2, t_2)f(x_2, t_2 | x_3, t_3)dx_2 \quad (4.1.7)$$

This equation can be used as the starting point for deriving the *Fokker-Planck equation* (see, e.g., [1] for details). First, equation (4.1.7) is transformed into the differential equation

$$\frac{\partial}{\partial t} f(x, t|x_0, t_0) = -\frac{\partial}{\partial x}[A(x, t)f(x, t|x_0, t_0)] + \frac{1}{2}\frac{\partial^2}{\partial x^2}[D(x, t)f(x, t|x_0, t_0)] +$$

$$\int [R(x|z, t)f(z, t|x_0, t_0) - R(z|x, t)f(x, t|x_0, t_0)]dz \quad (4.1.8)$$

In (4.1.8), the drift coefficient $A(x, t)$ and the diffusion coefficient $D(x, t)$ are equal

$$A(x, t) = \lim_{\Delta t \to 0} \frac{1}{\Delta t} \int (z - x)f(z, t + \Delta t|x, t)dz \quad (4.1.9)$$

$$D(x, t) = \lim_{\Delta t \to 0} \frac{1}{\Delta t} \int (z - x)^2 f(z, t + \Delta t|x, t)dz \quad (4.1.10)$$

The integral in the right-hand side of the Chapmen-Kolmogorov equation (4.1.8) is determined with the function

$$R(x|z, t) = \lim_{\Delta t \to 0} \frac{1}{\Delta t} f(x, t + \Delta t|z, t) \quad (4.1.11)$$

It describes possible *discontinuous jumps* of the random variable. Neglecting this term in equation (4.1.8) yields the Fokker-Planck equation

$$\frac{\partial}{\partial t} f(x, t|x_0, t_0) = -\frac{\partial}{\partial x}[A(x, t)f(x, t|x_0, t_0)]$$
$$+ \frac{1}{2}\frac{\partial^2}{\partial x^2}[D(x, t)f(x, t|x_0, t_0)] \quad (4.1.12)$$

This equation with $A(x, t) = 0$ and $D = $ const is reduced to the diffusion equation that describes the *Brownian motion*

$$\frac{\partial}{\partial t} f(x, t|x_0, t_0) = \frac{D}{2}\frac{\partial^2}{\partial x^2} f(x, t|x_0, t_0) \quad (4.1.13)$$

Equation (4.1.13) has the analytic solution in the Gaussian form

$$f(x, t|x_0, t_0) = [2\pi D(t - t_0)]^{-1/2} \exp[-(x - x_0)^2/2D(t - t_0)] \quad (4.1.14)$$

Mean and variance for the distribution (4.1.14) equal

$$E[x(t)] = x_0, \quad Var[x(t)] = E[(x(t) - x_0)^2] = \sigma^2 = D(t - t_0) \quad (4.1.15)$$

The diffusion equation (4.1.13) with $D = 1$ describes the *standard Wiener process* for which

$$E[(x(t) - x_0)^2] = t - t_0 \quad (4.1.16)$$

The notions of the generic Wiener process and the Brownian motion are sometimes used interchangeably, though there are some fine differences in their definitions [2, 3]. I shall denote the Wiener process with W(t) and reserve this term for the standard version (4.1.16), as it is often done in the literature.

The Brownian motion is the classical topic of statistical physics. Different approaches for introducing this process are described in the next section.

4.2 BROWNIAN MOTION

In mathematical statistics, the notion of the Brownian motion is used for describing the generic stochastic process. Yet, this term referred originally to Brown's observation of random motion of pollen in water. Random particle motion in fluid can be described using different theoretical approaches. Einstein's original theory of the Brownian motion implicitly employs both the Chapman-Kolmogorov equation and the Fokker-Planck equation [1]. However, choosing either one of these theories as the starting point can lead to the diffusion equation. Langevin offered another simple method for deriving the Fokker-Planck equation. He considered one-dimensional motion of a spherical particle of mass m and radius R that is subjected to two forces. The first force is the viscous drag force described by the Stokes formula, $\mathbf{F} = -6\pi\eta R\mathbf{v}$, where η is viscosity and $\mathbf{v} = \dfrac{d\mathbf{r}}{dt}$ is the particle velocity. Another force, $\mathbf{Z}$, describes collisions of the water molecules with the particle and therefore has a random nature. The *Langevin equation* of the particle motion is

$$m\frac{d\mathbf{v}}{dt} = -6\pi\eta R\mathbf{v} + \mathbf{Z} \qquad (4.2.1)$$

Let us multiply both sides of equation (4.2.1) by $\mathbf{r}$. Since $\mathbf{r}\dfrac{d\mathbf{v}}{dt} = \dfrac{d}{dt}(\mathbf{rv}) - \mathbf{v}^2$ and $\mathbf{rv} = \dfrac{1}{2}\dfrac{d}{dt}(\mathbf{r}^2)$, then

$$\frac{1}{2}m\frac{d^2}{dt^2}(\mathbf{r}^2) - m\left(\frac{d\mathbf{r}}{dt}\right)^2 = -3\pi\eta R\frac{d}{dt}(\mathbf{r}^2) + \mathbf{Zr} \qquad (4.2.2)$$

Note that the mean kinetic energy of a spherical particle, $E[\frac{1}{2}m\mathbf{v}^2]$, equals $\frac{3}{2}kT$. Since $E[\mathbf{Zr}] = 0$ due to the random nature of $\mathbf{Z}$, averaging of equation (4.2.2) yields

$$m \frac{d^2}{dt^2} E[\mathbf{r}^2] + 6\pi\eta R \frac{d}{dt} E[\mathbf{r}^2] = 6kT \qquad (4.2.3)$$

The solution to equation (4.2.3) is

$$\frac{d}{dt} E[\mathbf{r}^2] = kT/(\pi\eta R) + C \exp(-6\pi\eta Rt/m) \qquad (4.2.4)$$

where C is an integration constant. The second term in equation (4.2.4) decays exponentially and can be neglected in the asymptotic solution. Then

$$E[\mathbf{r}^2] - \mathbf{r}_0^2 = [kT/(\pi\eta R)]t \qquad (4.2.5)$$

where $\mathbf{r}_0$ is the particle position at $t = 0$. It follows from the comparison of equations (4.2.5) and (4.1.15) that $D = kT/(\pi\eta R)$.[1]

The Brownian motion can be also derived as the continuous limit for *the discrete random walk* (see, e.g., [3]). First, let us introduce the process $\varepsilon(t)$ that is named *the white noise* and satisfies the following conditions

$$E[\varepsilon(t)] = 0; \ E[\varepsilon^2(t)] = \sigma^2; \ E[\varepsilon(t) \ \varepsilon(s)] = 0, \text{ if } t \neq s. \qquad (4.2.6)$$

Hence, the white noise has zero mean and constant variance σ^2. The last condition in (4.2.6) implies that there is no linear correlation between different observations of the white noise. Such a model represents *an independently and identically distributed process (IID)* and is sometimes denoted IID(0, σ^2). The IID process can still have non-linear correlations (see Section 5.3). The normal distribution N(0, σ^2) is the special case of the white noise. First, consider a simple discrete process

$$y(k) = y(k - 1) + \varepsilon(k) \qquad (4.2.7)$$

where the white noise innovations can take only two values[2]

$$\varepsilon(k) = \begin{cases} \Delta, & \text{with probability p, p} = \text{const} < 1 \\ -\Delta, & \text{with probability } (1 - p) \end{cases} \qquad (4.2.8)$$

Now, let us introduce the continuous process $y_n(t)$ within the time interval $t \in [0, T]$, such that

$$y_n(t) = y([t/h]) = y([nt/T]), \ t \in [0, T] \qquad (4.2.9)$$

In (4.2.9), [x] denotes the greatest integer that does not exceed x. The process $y_n(t)$ has the stepwise form: it is constant except the moments $t = kh$, $k = 1, \ldots, n$. Mean and variance of the process $y_n(T)$ equal

$$E[y_n(T)] = n(2p - 1)\Delta = T(2p - 1)\Delta/h \qquad (4.2.10)$$

$$\mathrm{Var}[y_n(T)] = n\Delta^2 = T\Delta^2/h \qquad (4.2.11)$$

Both mean (4.2.10) and variance (4.2.11) become infinite in the limiting case $h \to 0$ with arbitrary Δ. Hence, we must impose a relation between Δ and h that ensures the finite values of the moments $E[y_n(T)]$ and $\mathrm{Var}[y_n(T)]$. Namely, let us set

$$p = (1 + \mu\sqrt{h}/\sigma)/2, \ \Delta = \sigma\sqrt{h} \qquad (4.2.12)$$

where μ and σ are some parameters. Then

$$E[y_n(T)] = \mu T, \ \mathrm{Var}[y_n(T)] = \sigma^2 T \qquad (4.2.13)$$

It can be shown that $y_n(T)$ converges to the normal distribution $N(\mu T, \sigma^2 T)$ in the continuous limit. Hence, μ and σ are the drift and diffusion parameters, respectively. Obviously, the drift parameter differs from zero only when $p \neq 0.5$, that is when there is preference for one direction of innovations over another. The continuous process defined with the relations (4.2.13) is named the *arithmetic Brownian motion*. It is reduced to the Wiener process when $\mu = 0$ and $\sigma = 1$.

Note that in a more generic approach, the time intervals between observations of y(t) themselves represent a random variable [4, 5]. While this process (so-called *continuous-time random walk*) better resembles the market price variations, its description is beyond the scope of this book.

In the general case, the arithmetic Brownian motion can be expressed in the following form

$$y(t) = \mu(t)t + \sigma(y(t), t)W(t) \qquad (4.2.14)$$

The random variable in this process may have negative values. This creates a problem for describing prices that are essentially positive. Therefore, the *geometric Brownian motion* $Y(t) = \exp[y(t)]$ is often used in financial applications.

One can simulate the Wiener process with the following equation

$$[W(t + \Delta t) - W(t)] \equiv \Delta W = N(0, 1)\sqrt{\Delta t} \qquad (4.2.15)$$

While the Wiener process is a continuous process, its innovations are random. Therefore, the limit of the expression $\Delta W / \Delta t$ does not converge when $\Delta t \rightarrow 0$. Indeed, it follows for the Wiener process that

$$\lim_{\Delta t \rightarrow 0} [\Delta W(t)/\Delta t] = \lim_{\Delta t \rightarrow 0} [\Delta t^{-1/2}] \qquad (4.2.16)$$

As a result, the derivative $dW(t)/dt$ does not exist in the ordinary sense. Thus, one needs a special calculus to describe the stochastic processes.

4.3 STOCHASTIC DIFFERENTIAL EQUATION

The Brownian motion (4.2.14) can be presented in the differential form[3]

$$dy(t) = \mu dt + \sigma dW(t) \qquad (4.3.1)$$

The equation (4.3.1) is named the *stochastic differential equation*. Note that the term $dW(t) = [W(t + dt) - W(t)]$ has the following properties

$$E[dW] = 0, \ E[dW \ dW] = dt, \ E[dW \ dt] = 0 \qquad (4.3.2)$$

Let us calculate $(dy)^2$ having in mind (4.3.2) and retaining the terms $O(dt)$:[4]

$$(dy)^2 = [\mu dt + \sigma dW]^2 = \mu^2 dt^2 + 2\mu dt \, \sigma dW + \sigma^2 dW^2 \approx \sigma^2 dt \quad (4.3.3)$$

It follows from (4.3.3) that while dy is a random variable, $(dy)^2$ is a deterministic one. This result allows one to derive the *Ito's lemma*. Consider a function $F(y, t)$ that depends on both deterministic, t, and stochastic, $y(t)$, variables. Let us expand the differential for $F(y, t)$ into the Taylor series retaining linear terms and bearing in mind equation (4.3.3)

$$dF(y, t) = \frac{\partial F}{\partial y} dy + \frac{\partial F}{\partial t} dt + \frac{1}{2} \frac{\partial^2 F}{\partial y^2} (dy)^2$$

$$= \frac{\partial F}{\partial y} dy + \left[\frac{\partial F}{\partial t} + \frac{\sigma^2}{2} \frac{\partial^2 F}{\partial y^2} \right] dt \qquad (4.3.4)$$

The Ito's expression (4.3.4) has an additional term in comparison with the differential for a function with deterministic independent variables. Namely, the term $\dfrac{\sigma^2}{2}\dfrac{\partial^2 F}{\partial y^2}$ dt has stochastic nature. If y(t) is the Brownian motion (4.3.1), then

$$dF(y, t) = \frac{\partial F}{\partial y}[\mu dt + \sigma dW(t)] + \left[\frac{\partial F}{\partial t} + \frac{\sigma^2}{2}\frac{\partial^2 F}{\partial y^2}\right]dt$$

$$= \left[\mu\frac{\partial F}{\partial y} + \frac{\partial F}{\partial t} + \frac{\sigma^2}{2}\frac{\partial^2 F}{\partial y^2}\right]dt + \sigma\frac{\partial F}{\partial y}dW(t) \qquad (4.3.5)$$

Let us consider the function $F = W^2$ as a simple example for employing the Ito's lemma. In this case, $\mu = 0$, $\sigma = 1$, and equation (4.3.5) is reduced to

$$dF = dt + 2WdW \qquad (4.3.6)$$

Finally, we specify the Ito's expression for the geometric Brownian motion $F = \exp[y(t)]$. Since in this case, $\dfrac{\partial F}{\partial y} = \dfrac{\partial^2 F}{\partial y^2} = F$ and $\dfrac{\partial F}{\partial t} = 0$, then

$$dF = \left[\mu + \frac{\sigma^2}{2}\right]Fdt + \sigma FdW(t) \qquad (4.3.7)$$

Hence, if F is the geometric Brownian motion, its relative change, dF/F, behaves as the arithmetic Brownian motion.

The Ito's lemma is a pillar of the option pricing theory. It will be used for deriving the classical Black-Scholes equation in Section 9.4.

4.4 STOCHASTIC INTEGRAL

Now that the stochastic differential has been introduced, let us discuss how to perform its integration. First, the *Riemann-Stieltjes integral* should be defined. Consider a deterministic function f(t) on the interval $t \in [0, T]$. In order to calculate the *Riemann integral* of f(t) over the interval [0, T], this interval is divided into n sub-intervals $t_0 = 0 < t_1 < \ldots < t_n = T$ and the following sum should be computed

$$S_n = \sum_{i=1}^{n} f(\tau_i)(t_i - t_{i-1}) \qquad (4.4.1)$$

where $\tau_i \in [t_{i-1}, t_i]$. The Riemann integral is the limit of S_n

$$\int_0^T f(t)dt = \lim S_n, \ \max(t_i - t_{i-1}) \to 0 \text{ for all } i. \tag{4.4.2}$$

Note that the limit (4.4.2) exists only if the function $f(t)$ is sufficiently smooth. Another type of integral is the *Stieltjes integral*. Let us define the differential of a function $g(x)$

$$dg = g(x + dx) - g(x) \tag{4.4.3}$$

Then the Stieltjes integral for the function $g(t)$ on the interval $t \in [0, T]$ is defined as

$$S_n = \sum_{i=1}^n f(\tau_i)[g(t_i) - g(t_{i-1})] \tag{4.4.4}$$

where $\tau_i \in [t_{i-1}, t_i]$

$$\int_0^T f(t)dg(t) = \lim S_n, \text{ where } \max(t_i - t_{i-1}) \to 0 \text{ for all } i. \tag{4.4.5}$$

If $g(t)$ has a derivative, then $dg \approx \dfrac{dg}{dt}dt = g'(t)dt$, and the sum (4.4.4) can be written as

$$S_n = \sum_{i=1}^n f(\tau_i)g'(\tau_i)(t_i - t_{i-1}) \tag{4.4.6}$$

Similarity between the Riemann sum (4.4.1) and the Stieltjes sum (4.4.6) leads to the definition of the Riemann-Stieltjes integral. The Riemann-Stieltjes integral over the deterministic functions does not depend on the particular choice of the point τ_i within the intervals $[t_{i-1}, t_i]$. However, if the function $f(t)$ is random, the sum S_n does depend on the choice of τ_i. Consider, for example, the sum (4.4.4) for the case $f(t) = g(t) = W(t)$ (where $W(t)$ is the Wiener process). It follows from (4.1.16) that

$$E[S_n] = E\left[\sum_{i=1}^n W(\tau_i)\{W(t_i) - W(t_{i-1})\}\right]$$

$$= \sum_{i=1}^n [\min(\tau_i, t_i) - \min(\tau_i, t_{i-1})] = \sum_{i=1}^n (\tau_i - t_{i-1}) \tag{4.4.7}$$

Let us set for all i

$$\tau_i = \alpha t_i + (1 - \alpha)t_{i-1} \quad 0 \leq \alpha \leq 1 \tag{4.4.8}$$

Substitution of (4.4.8) into (4.4.7) leads to $E[S_n] = \alpha T$. Hence, the sum (4.4.7) depends on the arbitrary parameter α and therefore can have any value. Within the Ito's formalism, the value $\alpha = 0$ is chosen, so that $\tau_i = t_{i-1}$. The *stochastic Ito's integral* is defined as

$$\int_0^T f(t)dW(t) = \text{ms-}\lim_{n \to \infty} \sum_{i=1}^n f(t_{i-1})[W(t_i) - W(t_{i-1})] \tag{4.4.9}$$

The notation ms-lim stands for the mean-square limit. It means that the difference between the Ito integral in the left-hand side of (4.4.9) and the sum in the right-hand side of (4.4.9) has variance that approaches zero as n increases to infinity. Thus, (4.4.9) is equivalent to

$$\lim_{n \to \infty} E\left[\int_0^T f(t)dW(t) - \sum_{i-1}^n f(t_{i-1})\{W(t_i) - W(t_{i-1})\}\right]^2 = 0 \tag{4.4.10}$$

Let us consider the integral

$$I(t_2, t_1) = \int_{t_1}^{t_2} W(t)dW(t) \tag{4.4.11}$$

as an example of calculating the Ito's integral. If the function $W(t)$ is deterministic, then the Riemann-Stieltjes integral $I_{R-S}(t_2, t_1)$ equals

$$I_{R-S}(t_2, t_1) = 0.5[W(t_2)^2 - W(t_1)^2] \tag{4.4.12}$$

However, when $W(t)$ is the Wiener process, the Ito's integral $I_I(t_2, t_1)$ leads to a somewhat unexpected result

$$I_I(t_2, t_1) = 0.5[W(t_2)^2 - W(t_1)^2 - (t_2 - t_1)] \tag{4.4.13}$$

This follows directly from equation (4.3.6). Obviously, the result (4.4.13) can be derived directly from the definition of the Ito's integral (see Exercise 1). Note that the mean of the Ito's integral (4.4.11) equals zero

$$E[I_I(t_2, t_1)] = 0 \tag{4.4.14}$$

The difference between the right-hand sides of (4.4.12) and (4.4.13) is determined by the particular choice of $\alpha = 0$ in (4.4.8). Stratonovich has offered another definition of the stochastic integral by choosing $\alpha = 0.5$. In contrast to equation (4.4.9), the *Stratonovich's integral* is defined as

$$\int_0^T f(t)dW(t) = ms-\lim_{n \to \infty} \sum_{i=1}^n f\left(\frac{t_{i-1} + t_i}{2}\right)[W(t_i) - W(t_{i-1})] \quad (4.4.15)$$

For the integrand in (4.4.11), the Stratonovich's integral $I_S(t_2, t_1)$ coincides with the Riemann-Stieltjes integral

$$I_S(t_2, t_1) = 0.5[W(t_2)^2 - W(t_1)^2] \quad (4.4.16)$$

Both Ito's and Stratonovich's formulations can be transformed into each other. In particular, the Ito's stochastic differential equation (4.3.1)

$$dy_I(t) = \mu dt + \sigma dW(t) \quad (4.4.17)$$

is equivalent to the Stratonovich's equation

$$dy_S(t) = \left[\mu - 0.5\sigma \frac{\partial \sigma}{\partial y}\right] dt + \sigma dW(t) \quad (4.4.18)$$

The applications of stochastic calculus in finance are based almost exclusively on the Ito's theory. Consider, for example, the integral

$$\int_{t_1}^{t_2} \sigma(t)dW(t) \quad (4.4.19)$$

If no correlation between the function $\sigma(t)$ and the innovation $dW(t)$ is assumed, then the Ito's approximation is a natural choice. In this case, the function $\sigma(t)$ is said to be a *nonanticipating function* [1, 2]. However, if the innovations $dW(t)$ are correlated (so-called *non-white noise*), then the Stratonovich's approximation appears to be an adequate theory [1, 6].

4.5 MARTINGALES

The martingale methodology plays an important role in the modern theory of finance [2, 7, 8]. *Martingale* is a stochastic process $X(t)$ that satisfies the following condition

$$E[X(t + 1)|X(t), X(t - 1), \ldots] = X(t) \qquad (4.5.1)$$

The equivalent definition is given by

$$E[X(t + 1) - X(t)|X(t), X(t - 1), \ldots] = 0 \qquad (4.5.2)$$

Both these definitions are easily generalized for the continuum presentation where the time interval, dt, between two sequent moments $t + 1$ and t approaches zero (dt → 0). The notion of martingale is rooted in the gambling theory. It is closely associated with the notion of *fair game*, in which none of the players has an advantage. The condition (4.5.1) implies that the expectation of the gamer wealth at time $t + 1$ conditioned on the entire history of the game is equal to the gamer wealth at time t. Similarly, equation (4.5.2) means that the expectation to win at every round of the game being conditioned on the history of the game equals zero. In other words, martingale has no trend. A process that has positive trend is named *submartingale*. A process with negative trend is called *supermartingale*.

The martingale hypothesis applied to the asset prices states that the expectation of future price is simply the current price. This assumption is closely related to the *Efficient Market Hypothesis* discussed in Section 2.3. Generally, the asset prices are not martingales for they incorporate risk premium. Indeed, there must be some reward offered to investors for bearing the risks associated with keeping the assets. It can be shown, however, that the prices with discounted risk premium are martingales [3].

The important property of the Ito's integral is that it is martingale. Consider, for example, the integral (4.4.19) approximated with the sum (4.4.9). Because the innovations dW(t) are unpredictable, it follows from (4.4.14) that

$$E\left[\int_t^{t+\Delta t} \sigma(z)dW(z)\right] = 0 \qquad (4.5.3)$$

Therefore,

$$E\left[\int_0^{t+\Delta t} \sigma(z)dW(z)\right] = \int_0^t \sigma(z)dW(z) \qquad (4.5.4)$$

and the integral (4.4.19) satisfies the martingale definition. Note that for the Brownian motion with drift (4.2.14)

$$E[y(t + dt)] = E\left[y(t) + \int_t^{t+dt} dy\right] = y(t) + \mu dt \qquad (4.5.5)$$

Hence, the Brownian motion with drift is not a martingale. However, the process

$$z(t) = y(t) - \mu t \qquad (4.5.6)$$

is a martingale since

$$E[z(t + dt)] = z(t) \qquad (4.5.7)$$

This result follows also from the *Doob-Meyer decomposition theorem*, which states that a continuous submartingale $X(t)$ at $0 \le t \le \infty$ with finite expectation $E[X(t)] < \infty$ can be decomposed into a continuous martingale and an increasing deterministic process.

4.6 REFERENCES FOR FURTHER READING

Theory and applications of the stochastic processes in natural sciences are described in [1, 6]. A good introduction to the stochastic calculus in finance is given in [2]. For a mathematically inclined reader, the presentation of the stochastic theory with increasing level of technical details can be found in [7, 8].

4.7 EXERCISES

1. Simulate daily price returns using the geometric Brownian motion (4.3.7) for four years. Use equation (4.2.15) for approximating ΔW. Assume that $S(0) = 10$, $\mu = 10\%$, $\sigma = 20\%$ (μ and σ are given per annum). Assume 250 working days per annum.
2. Prove that

$$\int_{t_1}^{t_2} W(s)^n dW(s) = \frac{1}{n+1}[W(t_2)^{n+1} - W(t_1)^{n+1}] - \frac{n}{2}\int_{t_1}^{t_2} W(s)^{n-1} ds$$

Hint: Calculate $d(W^{n+1})$ *using the Ito's lemma.*

3. Solve the *Ornstein-Uhlenbeck equation* that describes the *mean-reverting process* in which the solution fluctuates around its mean

$$dX = -\mu X dt + \sigma dW, \ \mu > 0$$

Hint: introduce the variable $Y = X \exp(\mu t)$.

*4. Derive the integral (4.4.13) directly from the definition of the Ito's integral (4.4.9).

Chapter 5

Time Series Analysis

Time series analysis has become an indispensable theoretical tool in financial and economic research. Section 5.1 is devoted to the commonly used univariate autoregressive and moving average models. The means for modeling trends and seasonality effects are described in Section 5.2. The processes with non-stationary variance (conditional heteroskedasticity) are discussed in Section 5.3. Finally, the specifics of the multivariate time series are introduced in Section 5.4.

5.1 AUTOREGRESSIVE AND MOVING AVERAGE MODELS

5.1.1 AUTOREGRESSIVE MODEL

First, we shall consider a *univariate time series* $y(t)$ for a process that is observed at moments $t = 0, 1, \ldots, n$ (see, e.g., [1, 2]). The time series in which the observation at moment t depends linearly on several lagged observations at moments $t - 1, t - 2, \ldots, t - p$

$$y(t) = a_1 y(t - 1) + a_2 y(t - 2) + \ldots + a_p y(t - p) + \varepsilon(t), \ t > p \quad (5.1.1)$$

is called the *autoregressive process* of order p, or AR(p). The term $\varepsilon(t)$ in (5.1.1) is the white noise that satisfies the conditions (4.2.6). The *lag operator* $L^p = y(t - p)$ is often used for describing time series. Note that $L^0 = y(t)$. Equation (5.1.1) in terms of the lag operator has the form

$$A_p(L)y(t) = \varepsilon(t) \tag{5.1.2}$$

where

$$A_p(L) = 1 - a_1 L - a_2 L^2 - \ldots - a_p L^p \tag{5.1.3}$$

The operator $A_p(L)$ is called the AR polynomial in lag operator of order p. Let us consider AR(1) that starts with a random shock. Its definition implies that

$$y(0) = \varepsilon(0), \ y(1) = a_1 y(0) + \varepsilon(1),$$

$$y(2) = a_1 y(1) + \varepsilon(2) = a_1{}^2 \varepsilon(0) + a_1 \varepsilon(1) + \varepsilon(2), \ldots$$

Hence, by induction,

$$y(t) = \sum_{i=0}^{t} a_1{}^i \varepsilon(t - i) \tag{5.1.4}$$

Mean and variance of AR(1) equal, respectively

$$E[y(t)] = 0, \ \text{Var}[y(t)] = \sigma^2 / (1 - a_1{}^2), \tag{5.1.5}$$

Obviously, the contributions of the "old" noise converge with time to zero when $|a_1| < 1$. As a result, this process does not drift too far from its mean. This feature is named *mean reversion*.

The process with $a_1 = 1$ is called *the random walk*

$$y(t) = y(t - 1) + \varepsilon(t) \tag{5.1.6}$$

In this case, equation (5.1.4) reduces to

$$y(t) = \sum_{i=0}^{t} \varepsilon(t - i)$$

The noise contributions to the random walk do not weaken with time. Therefore, the random walk does not exhibit mean reversion. Now, consider the process that represents the first difference

$$x(t) = y(t) - y(t - 1) = \varepsilon(t) \tag{5.1.7}$$

Obviously, past noise has only transitory character for the process $x(t)$. Therefore, $x(t)$ is mean-reverting. Some processes must be differenced several times in order to exclude non-transitory noise shocks. The processes differenced d times are named *integrated of order* d and denoted as I(d). The differencing operator is used for describing an I(d) process

$$\Delta_i^d = (1 - L^i)^d, \; j, \; d = \ldots, -2, -1, 0, 1, 2 \ldots \tag{5.1.8}$$

If an I(d) process can be reduced to AR(p) process while applying the differencing operator, it is named ARI(p, d) process and has the form:

$$\Delta_1^d y(t) - a_1 \Delta_1^d y(t-1) - \ldots - a_p \Delta_1^d y(t-p) = \varepsilon(t), \; t \geq p + d \tag{5.1.9}$$

Note that differencing a time series d times reduces the number of independent variables by d, so that the total number of independent variables in ARI(p, d) within the sample with n observations equals $n - p - d$.

The *unit root* is another notion widely used for discerning permanent and transitory effects of random shocks. It is based on the roots of the characteristic polynomial for the AR(p) model. For example, AR(1) has the characteristic polynomial

$$1 - a_1 z = 0 \tag{5.1.10}$$

If $a_1 = 1$, then $z = 1$ and the characteristic polynomial has the unit root. In general, the characteristic polynomial roots can have complex values. The solution to equation (5.1.10) is outside the unit circle (i.e., $z > 1$) when $a_1 < 1$. It can be shown that all solutions for AR(p) are outside the unit circle when

$$1 - a_1 z - a_2 z^2 - \ldots - a_p z^p = 0 \tag{5.1.11}$$

5.1.2 MOVING AVERAGE MODELS

A model more general than AR(p) contains both lagged observations and lagged noise

$$y(t) = a_1 y(t-1) + a_2 y(t-2) + \ldots + a_p y(t-p) + \varepsilon(t)$$
$$+ b_1 \varepsilon(t-1) + b_2 \varepsilon(t-2) + \ldots + b_q \varepsilon(t-q) \tag{5.1.12}$$

This model is called *autoregressive moving average model* of order (p,q), or simply ARMA(p,q). Sometimes modeling of empirical data requires AR(p) with a rather high number p. Then, ARMA(p, q) may be more efficient in that the total number of its terms (p + q) needed for given accuracy is lower than the number p in AR(p). ARMA(p, q) can be expanded into the integrated model, ARIMA(p, d, q), similar to the expansion of AR(p) into ARI(p, d). Neglecting the autoregressive terms in ARMA(p, q) yields a "pure" *moving average model* MA(q)

$$y(t) = \varepsilon(t) + b_1\varepsilon(t - 1) + b_2\varepsilon(t - 2) + \ldots + b_q\varepsilon(t - q) \qquad (5.1.13)$$

MA(q) can be presented in the form

$$y(t) = B_q(L)\varepsilon(t) \qquad (5.1.14)$$

where $B_q(L)$ is the MA polynomial in lag operator

$$B_q(L) = 1 + b_1L + b_2L^2 + \ldots + b_qL^q \qquad (5.1.15)$$

The moving average model does not depend explicitly on the lagged values of y(t). Yet, it is easy to show that this model implicitly incorporates the past. Consider, for example, the MA(1) model

$$y(t) = \varepsilon(t) + b_1\varepsilon(t - 1) \qquad (5.1.16)$$

with $\varepsilon(0) = 0$. For this model,

$$y(1) = \varepsilon(1), \; y(2) = \varepsilon(2) + b_1\varepsilon(1) = \varepsilon(2) + b_1y(1),$$
$$y(3) = \varepsilon(3) + b_1\varepsilon(2) = \varepsilon(3) + b_1(y(2) - b_1y(1)), \ldots$$

Thus, the general result for MA(1) has the form

$$y(t)(1 - b_1L + b_1L^2 - b_1L^3 + \ldots) = \varepsilon(t) \qquad (5.1.17)$$

Equation (5.1.17) can be viewed as the AR(∞) process, which illustrates that the MA model does depend on past.

The MA(q) model is *invertible* if it can be transformed into an AR(∞) model. It can be shown that MA(q) is invertible if all solutions to the equation

$$1 + b_1z + b_2z^2 + \ldots + b_qz^q = 0 \qquad (5.1.18)$$

are outside the unit circle. In particular, MA(1) is invertible if $|b_1| < 1$. If the process y(t) has a non-zero mean value m, then the AR(1) model can be presented in the following form

$$y(t) - m = a_1[y(t-1) - m] + \varepsilon(t) = c + a_1 y(t-1) + \varepsilon(t) \quad (5.1.19)$$

In (5.1.19), intercept c equals:

$$c = m(1 - a_1) \quad (5.1.20)$$

The general AR(p) model with a non-zero mean has the following form

$$A_p(L)y(t) = c + \varepsilon(t), \ c = m(1 - a_1 - \ldots a_p) \quad (5.1.21)$$

Similarly, the intercept can be included into the general moving average model MA(q)

$$y(t) = c + B_p(L)\varepsilon(t), \ c = m \quad (5.1.22)$$

Note that mean of the MA model coincides with its intercept because mean of the white noise is zero.

5.1.3 AUTOCORRELATION AND FORECASTING

Now, let us introduce the *autocorrelation function (ACF)* for process y(t)

$$\rho(k) = \gamma(k)/\gamma(0) \quad (5.1.23)$$

where $\gamma(k)$ is the *autocovariance* of order k

$$\gamma(k) = E[y(t) - m)(y(t-k) - m)] \quad (5.1.24)$$

The autocorrelation functions may have some typical patterns, which can be used for identification of empirical time series [2]. The obvious properties of ACF are

$$\rho(0) = 1, \ -1 < \rho(k) < 1 \text{ for } k \neq 0 \quad (5.1.25)$$

ACF is closely related to the ARMA parameters. In particular, for AR(1)

$$\rho(1) = a_1 \quad (5.1.26)$$

The ACF of the first order for MA(1) equals

$$\rho(1) = b_1/(b_1^2 + 1) \quad (5.1.27)$$

The right-hand side of the expression (5.1.27) has the same value for the inverse transform $b_1 \rightarrow 1/b_1$. For example, two processes

$$x(t) = \varepsilon(t) + 2\varepsilon(t - 1)$$
$$y(t) = \varepsilon(t) + 0.5\varepsilon(t - 1)$$

have the same $\rho(1)$. Note, however, that $y(t)$ is an invertible process while $x(t)$ is not.

ARMA modeling is widely used for forecasting. Consider a forecast of a variable $y(t + 1)$ based on a set of n variables $x(t)$ known at moment t. This set can be just past values of y, that is, $y(t), y(t - 1), \ldots, y(t - n + 1)$. Let us denote the forecast with $\hat{y}(t + 1|t)$. The quality of forecast is usually defined with the some loss function. The *mean squared error (MSE)* is the conventional loss function in many applications

$$\text{MSE}(\hat{y}(t + 1|t)) = E[(y(t + 1) - \hat{y}(t + 1|t))^2] \qquad (5.1.28)$$

The forecast that yields the minimum of MSE turns out to be the expectation of $y(t + 1)$ conditioned on $x(t)$

$$\hat{y}(t + 1|t) = E[y(t + 1)|x(t)] \qquad (5.1.29)$$

In the case of linear regression

$$y(t + 1) = \mathbf{b}'\mathbf{x}(t) + \varepsilon(t) \qquad (5.1.30)$$

MSE is reduced to the *ordinary least squares (OLS)* estimate for $\mathbf{b}$. For a sample with T observations,

$$\mathbf{b} = \sum_{t=1}^{T} \mathbf{x}(t)y(t + 1) / \sum_{t=1}^{T} \mathbf{x}(t)\mathbf{x}'(t) \qquad (5.1.31)$$

Another important concept in the time series analysis is the *maximum likelihood estimate (MLE)* [2]. Consider the general ARMA model (5.1.12) with the white noise (4.2.6). The problem is how to estimate the ARMA parameters on the basis of given observations of $y(t)$. The idea of MLE is to find such a vector $\mathbf{r}' = (a_1, \ldots, a_p, \ldots, b_1, \ldots, b_q, \sigma^2)$ that maximizes the likelihood function for given observations $(y_1, y_2, \ldots, y_T)$

$$f_{1, 2, \ldots, T}(y_1, y_2, \ldots, y_T; \mathbf{r}') \qquad (5.1.32)$$

The likelihood function (5.1.32) has the sense of probability of observing the data sample $(y_1, y_2, \ldots, y_T)$. In this approach, the ARMA model and the probability distribution for the white noise should be specified first. Often the normal distribution leads to reasonable estimates even if the real distribution is different. Furthermore, the likelihood function must be calculated for the chosen ARMA model. Finally, the components of the vector **r′** must be estimated. The latter step may require sophisticated numerical optimization technique. Details of implementation of MLE are discussed in [2].

5.2 TRENDS AND SEASONALITY

Finding trends is an important part of the time series analysis. Presence of trend implies that the time series has no mean reversion. Moreover, mean and variance of a trending process depend on the sample. The time series with trend is named *non-stationary*. If a process y(t) is *stationary*, its mean, variance, and autocovariance are finite and do not depend on time. This implies that autocovariance (5.1.24) depends only on the lag parameter k. Such a definition of stationarity is also called *covariance-stationarity* or *weak stationarity* because it does not impose any restrictions on the higher moments of the process. *Strict stationarity* implies that higher moments also do not depend on time. Note that any MA process is covariance-stationary. However, the AR(p) process is covariance-stationary only if the roots of its polynomial are outside the unit circle.

It is important to discern *deterministic trend* and *stochastic trend*. They have a different nature yet their graphs may look sometimes very similar [1]. Consider first the AR(1) model with the deterministic trend

$$y(t) - m - ct = a_1(y(t-1) - m - c(t-1)) + \varepsilon(t) \qquad (5.2.1)$$

Let us introduce $z(t) = y(t) - m - ct$. Then equation (5.2.1) has the solution

$$z(t) = a_1{}^t z(0) + \sum_{i=1}^{t} a_1{}^{t-i} \varepsilon(t) \qquad (5.2.2)$$

where z(0) is a pre-sample starting value of z. Obviously, the random shocks are transitory if $|a_1| < 1$. The trend incorporated in the definition of z(t) is deterministic when $|a_1| < 1$. However, if $a_1 = 1$, then equation (5.2.1) has the form

$$y(t) = c + y(t - 1) + \varepsilon(t) \qquad (5.2.3)$$

The process (5.2.3) is named the *random walk with drift*. In this case, equation (5.2.2) is reduced to

$$z(t) = z(0) + \sum_{i=1}^{t} \varepsilon(t) \qquad (5.2.4)$$

The sum of non-transitory shocks in the right-hand side of equation (5.2.4) is named *stochastic trend*. Consider, for example, the deterministic trend model with m = 0 and $\varepsilon(t) = N(0, 1)$

$$y(t) = 0.1t + \varepsilon(t) \qquad (5.2.5)$$

and the stochastic trend model

$$y(t) = 0.1 + y(t - 1) + \varepsilon(t), \; y(0) = 0 \qquad (5.2.6)$$

As it can be seen from Figure 5.1, both graphs look similar. In general, however, the stochastic trend model can deviate from the deterministic trend for a long time.

Stochastic trend implies that the process is I(1). Then the lag polynomial (5.1.3) can be represented in the form

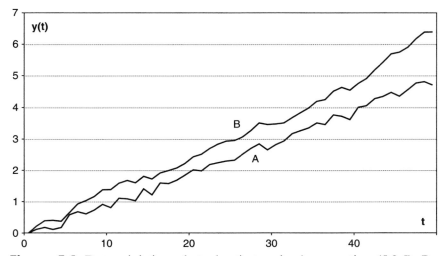

Figure 5.1 Deterministic and stochastic trends: A - equation (5.2.5), B - equation (5.2.6).

$$A_p(L) = (1 - L)A_{p-1}(L) \qquad (5.2.7)$$

Similarly, the process I(2) has the lag polynomial

$$A_p(L) = (1 - L)^2 A_{p-2}(L) \qquad (5.2.8)$$

and so on. The standard procedure for testing presence of the unit root in time series is the Dickey-Fuller method [1, 2]. This method is implemented in major econometric software packages (see the Section 5.5).

Seasonal effects may play an important role in the properties of time series. Sometimes, there is a need to eliminate these effects in order to focus on the stochastic specifics of the process. Various differencing filters can be used for achieving this goal [2]. In other cases, seasonal effect itself may be the object of interest. The general approach for handling seasonal effects is introducing *dummy parameters* D(s, t) where s = 1, 2, ..., S; S is the number of seasons. For example, S = 12 is used for modeling the monthly effects. Then the parameter D(s, t) equals 1 at a specific season s and equals zero at all other seasons. The seasonal extension of an ARMA(p,q) model has the following form

$$y(t) = a_1 y(t - 1) + a_2 y(t - 2) + \ldots + a_p y(t - p) + \varepsilon(t)$$

$$+ b_1 \varepsilon(t - 1) + b_2 \varepsilon(t - 2) + \ldots + b_q \varepsilon(t - q) + \sum_{s=1}^{S} d_s D(s, t) \qquad (5.2.9)$$

Note that forecasting with the model (5.2.9) requires estimating (p + q + S) parameters.

5.3 CONDITIONAL HETEROSKEDASTICITY

So far, we considered random processes with the white noise (4.2.6) that are characterized with constant unconditional variance. Conditional variance has not been discussed so far. In general, the processes with unspecified conditional variance are named *homoskedastic*. Many random time series are not well described with the IID process. In particular, there may be strong positive autocorrelation in squared asset returns. This means that large returns (either positive or negative) follow large returns. In this case, it is said that the return volatility is clustered. The effect of volatility clustering is also called *autoregressive conditional heteroskedasticity (ARCH)*. It should be noted that small autocorrelation in squared returns does not necessarily mean that there is no volatility clustering. Strong outliers that lead to high values of skewness and kurtosis may lower autocorrelation. If these outliers are removed from the sample, volatility clustering may become apparent [3].

Several models in which past shocks contribute to the current volatility have been developed. Generally, they are rooted in the ARCH(m) model where the conditional variance is a weighed sum of m squared lagged returns

$$\sigma^2(t) = \omega + a_1\varepsilon^2(t-1) + a_2\varepsilon^2(t-2) + \ldots + a_m\varepsilon^2(t-m) \quad (5.3.1)$$

In (5.3.1), $\varepsilon(t) \sim N(0, \sigma^2(t))$, $\omega > 0$, $a_1, \ldots, a_m \geq 0$. Unfortunately, application of the ARCH(m) process to modeling the financial time series often requires polynomials with high order m. A more efficient model is the *generalized ARCH (GARCH)* process. The GARCH (m, n) process combines the ARCH(m) process with the AR(n) process for lagged variance

$$\sigma^2(t) = \omega + a_1\varepsilon^2(t-1) + a_2\varepsilon^2(t-2) + \ldots + a_m\varepsilon^2(t-m)$$
$$+ b_1\sigma^2(t-1) + b_2\sigma^2(t-2) + \ldots + b_n\sigma^2(t-n) \quad (5.3.2)$$

The simple GARCH(1, 1) model is widely used in applications

$$\sigma^2(t) = \omega + a\varepsilon^2(t-1) + b\sigma^2(t-1) \quad (5.3.3)$$

Equation (5.3.3) can be transformed into

$$\sigma^2(t) = \omega + (a+b)\sigma^2(t-1) + a[\varepsilon^2(t) - \sigma^2(t-1)] \quad (5.3.4)$$

The last term in equation (5.3.4) is conditioned on information available at time $(t-1)$ and has zero mean. This term can be treated as a shock to volatility. Therefore, the unconditional expectation of volatility for the GARCH(1, 1) model equals

$$E[\sigma^2(t)] = \omega/(1 - a - b) \quad (5.3.5)$$

This implies that the GARCH(1, 1) process is weakly stationary when $a + b < 1$. The advantage of the stationary GARCH(1, 1) model is that it can be easily used for forecasting. Namely, the conditional expectation of volatility at time $(t + k)$ equals [4]

$$E[\sigma^2(t+k)] = (a+b)^k[\sigma^2(t) - \omega/(1-a-b)] + \omega/(1-a-b) \quad (5.3.6)$$

The GARCH(1, 1) model (5.3.4) can be rewritten as

$$\sigma^2(t) = \omega/(1-b) + a(\varepsilon^2(t-1) + b\varepsilon^2(t-2) + b^2\varepsilon^2(t-3) + \ldots) \quad (5.3.7)$$

Equation (5.3.7) shows that the GARCH(1, 1) model is equivalent to the infinite ARCH model with exponentially weighed coefficients. This explains why the GARCH models are more efficient than the ARCH models.

Several GARCH models have been described in the econometric literature [1–3]. One popular GARCH(1, 1) model with $a + b = 1$ is called *integrated GARCH* (IGARCH). It has the autoregressive unit root. Therefore volatility of this process follows random walk and can be easily forecasted

$$E[\sigma^2(t+k)] = \sigma^2(t) + k\omega \quad (5.3.8)$$

IGARCH can be presented in the form

$$\sigma^2(t) = \omega + (1-\lambda)\varepsilon^2(t-1) + \lambda\sigma^2(t-1) \quad (5.3.9)$$

where $0 < \lambda < 1$. If $\omega = 0$, IGARCH coincides with the *exponentially weighed moving average (EWMA)*

$$\sigma^2(t) = (1-\lambda)\sum_{i=1}^{n}\lambda^{i-1}\varepsilon^2(t-i) \quad (5.3.10)$$

Indeed, the n-period EWMA for a time series y(t) is defined as

$$z(t) = [y(t-1) + \lambda y(t-2) + \lambda^2 y(t-3) + \ldots + \\ \lambda^{n-1}y(t-n)]/(1+\lambda+\ldots+\lambda^n) \quad (5.3.11)$$

where $0 < \lambda < 1$. For large n, the denominator of (5.3.11) converges to $1/(1-\lambda)$. Then for $z(t) = \sigma^2(t)$ and $y(t) = \varepsilon^2(t)$, equation (5.3.11) is equivalent to equation (5.3.7) with $\omega = 0$.

The GARCH models discussed so far are symmetric in that the shock sign does not affect the resulting volatility. In practice, however, negative price shocks influence volatility more than the positive shocks. A noted example of the asymmetric GARCH model is the *exponential GARCH (EGARCH)* (see, e.g., [3]). It has the form

$$\log[\sigma^2(t)] = \omega + \beta\log[\sigma^2(t-1)] + \lambda z(t-1) + \\ \gamma(|z(t-1)| - \sqrt{2/\pi}) \quad (5.3.12)$$

where $z(t) = \varepsilon(t)/\sigma(t)$. Note that $E[z(t)] = \sqrt{2/\pi}$. Hence, the last term in (5.3.12) is the mean deviation of $z(t)$. If $\gamma > 0$ and $\lambda < 0$, negative shocks lead to higher volatility than positive shocks.

5.4 MULTIVARIATE TIME SERIES

Often the current value of a variable depends not only on its past values, but also on past and/or current values of other variables. Modeling of dynamic interdependent variables is conducted with *multivariate time series*. The multivariate models yield not only new implementation problems but also some methodological difficulties. In particular, one should be cautious with simple regression models

$$y(t) = ax(t) + \varepsilon(t) \qquad (5.4.1)$$

that may lead to spurious results. It is said that (5.4.1) is a *simultaneous equation* as both explanatory (x) and dependent (y) variables are present at the same moment of time. A notorious example for spurious inference is the finding that the best predictor in the United Nations database for the Standard & Poor's 500 stock index is production of butter in Bangladesh [5].

A statistically sound yet spurious relationship is named *data snooping*. It may appear when the data being the subject of research are used to construct the test statistics [4]. Another problem with simultaneous equations is that noise can be correlated with the explanatory variable, which leads to inaccurate OLS estimates of the regression coefficients. Several techniques for handling this problem are discussed in [2].

A multivariate time series $y(t) = (y_1(t), y_2(t), \ldots, y_n(t))'$ is a vector of n processes that have data available for the same moments of time. It is supposed also that all these processes are either stationary or have the same order of integration. In practice, the multivariate moving average models are rarely used due to some restrictions [1]. Therefore, we shall focus on the *vector autoregressive model (VAR)* that is a simple extension of the univariate AR model to multivariate time series. Consider a bivariate VAR(1) process

$$y_1(t) = a_{10} + a_{11}y_1(t-1) + a_{12}y_2(t-1) + \varepsilon_1(t)$$
$$y_2(t) = a_{20} + a_{21}y_1(t-1) + a_{22}y_2(t-1) + \varepsilon_2(t) \qquad (5.4.2)$$

that can be presented in the matrix form

$$y(t) = \mathbf{a}_0 + \mathbf{A}y(t-1) + \boldsymbol{\varepsilon}(t) \tag{5.4.3}$$

In (5.4.3), $y(t) = (y_1(t), y_2(t))'$, $\mathbf{a}_0 = (a_{10}, a_{20})'$, $\boldsymbol{\varepsilon}(t) = (\varepsilon_1(t), \varepsilon_2(t))'$,
and $\mathbf{A} = \begin{bmatrix} a_{11} & a_{12} \\ a_{21} & a_{22} \end{bmatrix}$.

The right-hand sides in example (5.4.2) depend on past values only. However, dependencies on current values can also be included (so-called simultaneous dynamic model [1]). Consider the modification of the bivariate process (5.4.2)

$$y_1(t) = a_{11}y_1(t-1) + a_{12}y_2(t) + \varepsilon_1(t)$$
$$y_2(t) = a_{21}y_1(t) + a_{22}y_2(t-1) + \varepsilon_2(t) \tag{5.4.4}$$

The matrix form of this process is

$$\begin{bmatrix} 1 & -a_{12} \\ -a_{21} & 1 \end{bmatrix} \begin{bmatrix} y_1(t) \\ y_2(t) \end{bmatrix} = \begin{bmatrix} a_{11} & 0 \\ 0 & a_{22} \end{bmatrix} \begin{bmatrix} y_1(t-1) \\ y_2(t-1) \end{bmatrix} + \begin{bmatrix} \varepsilon_1(t) \\ \varepsilon_2(t) \end{bmatrix} \tag{5.4.5}$$

Multiplying both sides of (5.4.5) with the inverse of the left-hand matrix yields

$$\begin{bmatrix} y_1(t) \\ y_2(t) \end{bmatrix} = (1 - a_{12}a_{21})^{-1} \begin{bmatrix} a_{11} & a_{12}a_{22} \\ a_{11}a_{21} & a_{22} \end{bmatrix} \begin{bmatrix} y_1(t-1) \\ y_2(t-1) \end{bmatrix}$$
$$+ (1 - a_{12}a_{21})^{-1} \begin{bmatrix} 1 & a_{12} \\ a_{21} & 1 \end{bmatrix} \begin{bmatrix} \varepsilon_1(t) \\ \varepsilon_2(t) \end{bmatrix} \tag{5.4.6}$$

Equation (5.4.6) shows that the simultaneous dynamic models can also be represented in the VAR form.

In the general case of n-variate time series, VAR(p) has the form [2]

$$y(t) = \mathbf{a}_0 + \mathbf{A_1}y(t-1) + \ldots + \mathbf{A_p}y(t-p) + \boldsymbol{\varepsilon}(t) \tag{5.4.7}$$

where $y(t)$, $\mathbf{a}_0$, and $\boldsymbol{\varepsilon}(t)$ are n-dimensional vectors and $\mathbf{A_i}(i = 1, \ldots, p)$ are n x n matrices. Generally, the white noises $\boldsymbol{\varepsilon}(t)$ are mutually independent. Let us introduce

$$\bar{\mathbf{A}}_p(L) = \mathbf{I}_n - \mathbf{A_1}L - \ldots - \mathbf{A_p}L^p \tag{5.4.8}$$

where $\mathbf{I}_n$ is the n-dimensional unit vector. Then equation (5.4.7) can be presented as

$$\bar{A}_p(L)y(t) = \mathbf{a}_0 + \boldsymbol{\varepsilon}(t) \qquad (5.4.9)$$

Two covariance-stationary processes $x(t)$ and $y(t)$ are jointly covariance-stationary if their covariance $Cov(x(t), y(t - s))$ depends on lag s only. The condition for the covariance-stationary VAR(p) is the generalization of (5.1.11) for AR(p). Namely, all values of z satisfying the equation

$$|\mathbf{I}_n - \mathbf{A}_1 z - \ldots - \mathbf{A}_p z^p| = 0 \qquad (5.4.10)$$

must lie outside the unit circle. Equivalently, all solutions of the equation

$$|\mathbf{I}_n \lambda^p - \mathbf{A}_1 \lambda^{p-1} - \ldots - \mathbf{A}_p| = 0 \qquad (5.4.11)$$

must satisfy the condition $|\lambda| < 1$.

The problem of whether the lagged values of process y can improve prediction of process x (so-called *Granger causality*) is often posed in forecasting. It is said that if y fails to Granger-cause x, then the following condition holds for all $s > 0$

$$MSE(E[x(t + s)|x(t), x(t - 1), \ldots]) =$$
$$MSE(E[x(t + s)|x(t), x(t - 1), \ldots, y(t), y(t - 1), \ldots]) \quad (5.4.12)$$

In this case, y is called *exogenous variable* with respect to x. For example, $y_2(t)$ is exogenous with respect to $y_1(t)$ in (5.4.2) if $a_{12} = 0$. General methods for testing the Granger causality are described in [2].

The last notion that is introduced in this section is *cointegration*. Two processes are cointegrated if they both have unit roots (i.e., they both are I(1)), but some linear combination of these processes is stationary (i.e., is I(0)). This definition can be extended to an arbitrary number of processes. As an example, consider a bivariate model

$$y_1(t) = a y_2(t) + \varepsilon_1(t)$$
$$y_2(t) = y_2(t - 1) + \varepsilon_2(t) \qquad (5.4.13)$$

Both processes $y_1(t)$ and $y_2(t)$ are random walks. However the process

$$z(t) = y_1(t) - a y_2(t) \qquad (5.4.14)$$

is stationary. Details of testing the integration hypothesis are described in [2]. Implications of cointegration in financial data analysis are discussed in [3].

5.5 REFERENCES FOR FURTHER READING AND ECONOMETRIC SOFTWARE

A good concise introduction into the time series analysis is given by Franses [1]. The comprehensive presentation of the subject can be found in monographs by Hamilton [2] and Green [6]. Important specifics of time series analysis in finance, particularly for analysis and forecasting of volatility, are discussed by Alexander in [3]. In this chapter, only time series on homogenous grids were considered. Specifics of analysis of tick-by-tick data on non-homogenous grids are discussed in [7]. It should be noted that the exercises with the econometric software packages are very helpful for learning the subject. Besides the generic scientific software such as SAS, Splus, and Matlab that have modules for the time series analysis, several econometric software packages are available: PCGive, RATS, Shazam, and TSP. While these packages may have the trial and student versions, Easy-Reg offered by H. J. Bierens[5] has sufficient capability for an introductory course and is free of charge.

5.6 EXERCISES

1. Verify equations (5.1.25)–(5.1.27).
2. Verify if the process $y(t) = 1.2y(t - 1) - 0.32y(t - 2) + \varepsilon(t)$ (where $\varepsilon(t)$ is IID) is covariance-stationary.
3. Estimate the linear dividend growth rate from the dividends paid in the last years (verify these data on the AMEX website: *http://www.amex.com*): 2000 – \$1.51, 2001 – \$1.42, 2002 – \$1.50, and 2003 – \$1.63.
4. Verify equation (5.4.6) for the processes (5.4.4).

Chapter 6

Fractals

In short, fractals are the geometric objects that are constructed by repeating geometric patterns at a smaller and smaller scale. The fractal theory is a beautiful theory that describes beautiful objects. Development of the fractal theory and its financial applications has been greatly influenced by Mandelbrot [1]. In this chapter, a short introduction to the fractal theory relevant to financial applications is given. In Section 6.1, the basic definitions of the fractal theory are provided. Section 6.2 is devoted to the concept of multifractals that has been receiving a lot of attention in the recent research of the financial time series.

6.1 BASIC DEFINITIONS

Self-similarity is the defining property of fractals. This property implies that the geometric patterns are isotropic, meaning shape transformations along all coordinate axes are the same. If the geometric patterns are not isotropic, say the object is contracted along the y-axis with a scale different from that of along the x-axis, it is said that the object is *self-affine*. The difference between self-similarity and self-affinity is obvious for geometric objects. However, only self-affinity is relevant for the graphs of financial time series [1]. Indeed, since time and prices are measured with different units, their scaling factors cannot be compared.

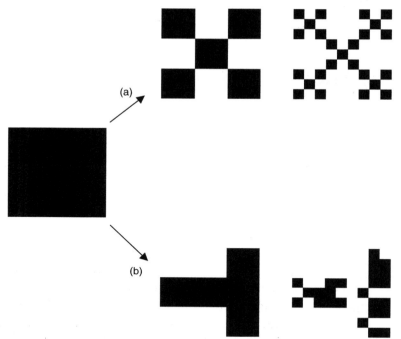

Figure 6.1 Deterministic (a) and stochastic (b) fractals with the same fractal dimension D = ln(5)/ln(3).

If the geometric pattern used in fractal design is deterministic, the resulting object is named a *deterministic fractal*. Consider an example in path (a) of Figure 6.1 where a square is repeatedly divided into nine small squares and four of them that have even numbers are deleted (the squares are numerated along rows). If four squares are deleted at random, one obtains a *random fractal* (one of such fractals is depicted in path (b) of Figure 6.1). While the deterministic and stochastic fractals in Figure 6.1 look quite different, they have the same *fractal dimension*. Let us outline the physical sense of this notion.

Consider a jagged line, such as a coastline. It is embedded into a plane. Thus, its dimension is lower than two. Yet, the more zigzagged the line is, the greater part of plane it covers. One may then expect that the dimension of a coastline is higher than one and it depends on a measure of jaggedness. Another widely used example is a crumpled paper ball. It is embedded in three-dimensional space. Yet, the volume of a paper ball depends on the sizes of its creases. Therefore, its dimension is expected to be in the range of two to three. Thus, we come to the notion of the fractal (non-integer) dimension for objects that cannot be accurately described within the framework of Euclidian geometry.

There are several technical definitions for the fractal dimension [2]. The most popular one is the *box-counting dimension*. It implies mapping the grid boxes of size h (e.g., squares and cubes for the two-dimensional and the three-dimensional spaces, respectively) onto the object of interest. The number of boxes that fill the object is $N(h) \sim h^{-D}$. The fractal dimension D is then the limit

$$D = \lim_{h \to 0} [\ln N(h)/\ln(1/h)] \qquad (6.1.1)$$

The box-counting dimension has another equivalent definition with the fixed unit size of the grid box and varying object size L

$$D = \lim_{L \to \infty} [\ln N(L)/\ln(L)] \qquad (6.1.2)$$

The fractal dimension for both deterministic and stochastic fractals in Figure 6.1 equals $D = \ln(5)/\ln(3) \approx 1.465$. Random fractals exhibit self-similarity only in a statistical sense. Therefore, the scale invariance is a more appropriate concept for random fractals than self-similarity.

The *iterated function systems* are commonly used for generating fractals. The two-dimensional iterated function algorithm for N fixed points can be presented as

$$X(k+1) = \rho X(k) + (1 - \rho) X_F(i)$$
$$Y(k+1) = \rho Y(k) + (1 - \rho) Y_F(i) \qquad (6.1.3)$$

In (6.1.3), ρ is the scaling parameter; $X_F(i)$ and $Y_F(i)$ are the coordinates of the fixed point i; $i = 1, 2, \ldots N$. The fixed point i is selected at every iteration at random. A famous example with $N = 3$, the Sierpinski triangle, is shown in Figure 6.2.

Now, let us turn to the random processes relevant to financial time series. If a random process X(t) is self-affine, then it satisfies the scaling rule

$$X(ct) = c^H X(t) \qquad (6.1.4)$$

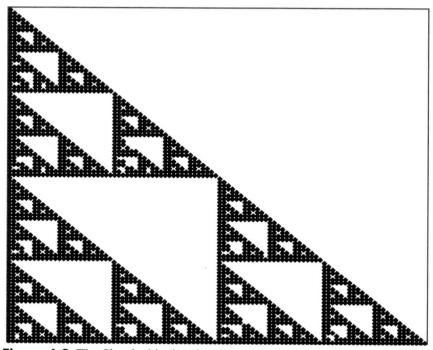

Figure 6.2 The Sierpinski triangle with $\rho = 0.5$.

The parameter H is named the *Hurst exponent*. Let us introduce the *fractional Brownian motion* $B_H(t)$. This random process satisfies the following conditions for all t and T [1]

$$E[B_H(t + T) - B_H(t)] = 0, \qquad (6.1.5)$$

$$E[B_H(t + T) - B_H(t)]^2 = T^{2H} \qquad (6.1.6)$$

When $H = \frac{1}{2}$, the fractional Brownian motion is reduced to the regular Brownian motion. For the Brownian motion, the correlation between the past average $E[B_H(t) - B_H(t - T)]/T$ and the future average $E[B_H(t + T) - B_H(t)]/T$ equals

$$C = 2^{2H-1} - 1 \qquad (6.1.7)$$

Obviously, this correlation does not depend on T. If $\frac{1}{2} < H < 1$, then $C > 0$ and it is said that $B_H(t)$ is a *persistent process*. Namely, if $B_H(t)$ grew in the past, it will most likely grow in the immediate future.

Conversely, if $B_H(t)$ decreased in the past, it will most probably continue to fall. Thus, persistent processes maintain trend. In the opposite case $(0 < H < \frac{1}{2}, C < 0)$, the process is named *anti-persistent*. It is said also that anti-persistent processes are mean reverting; for example, if the current process innovation is positive, then the next one will most likely be negative, and vice versa. There is a simple relationship between the box-counting fractal dimension and the Hurst exponent

$$D = 2 - H \qquad (6.1.8)$$

The fractal dimension of a time series can be estimated using the Hurst's *rescaled range (R/S) analysis* [1, 3]. Consider the data set $x_i (i = 1, \dots N)$ with mean m_N and the standard deviation σ_N. To define the rescaled range, the partial sums S_k must be calculated

$$S_k = \sum_{i=1}^{k} (x_i - m_N),\ 1 \leq k \leq N \qquad (6.1.9)$$

The rescaled range equals

$$R/S = [\max{(S_k)} - \min{(S_k)}]/\sigma_N,\ 1 \leq k \leq N \qquad (6.1.10)$$

The value of R/S is always greater than zero since $\max{(S_k)} > 0$ and $\min{(S_k)} < 0$. For given R/S, the Hurst exponent can be estimated using the relation

$$R/S = (aN)^H \qquad (6.1.11)$$

where a is a constant. The R/S analysis is superior to many other methods of determining long-range dependencies. But this approach has a noted shortcoming, namely, high sensitivity to the short-range memory [4].

6.2 MULTIFRACTALS

Let us turn to the generic notion of *multifractals* (see, e.g., [5]). Consider the map filled with a set of boxes that are used in the box-counting fractal dimension. What matters for the fractal concept is whether the given box belongs to fractal. The basic idea behind the notion of multifractals is that every box is assigned a measure μ that characterizes some probability density (e.g., intensity of color between the white and black limits). The so-called multiplicative process (or *cascade*) defines the rule according to which measure is fragmented when the object is partitioned into smaller components. The fragmentation ratios that are used in this process are named *multipliers*. The multifractal measure is characterized with the *Hölder exponent* α

$$\alpha = \lim_{h \to 0} [\ln \mu(h) / \ln (h)] \qquad (6.2.1)$$

where h is the box size. Let us denote the number of boxes with given h and α via $N_h(\alpha)$. The distribution of the Hölder exponents in the limit $h \to 0$ is sometimes called the *multifractal spectrum*

$$f(\alpha) = - \lim_{h \to 0} [\ln N_h(\alpha) / \ln (h)] \qquad (6.2.2)$$

The distribution $f(\alpha)$ can be treated as a generalization of the fractal dimension for the multifractal processes.

Let us describe the simplest multifractal, namely the *binomial measure* μ on the interval [0, 1] (see [5] for details). In the binomial cascade, two positive multipliers, m_0 and m_1, are chosen so that $m_0 + m_1 = 1$. At the step $k = 0$, the uniform probability measure for mass distribution, $\mu_0 = 1$, is used. At the next step ($k = 1$), the measure μ_1 uniformly spreads mass in proportion m_0 / m_1 on the intervals [0, $\frac{1}{2}$] and [$\frac{1}{2}$, 1], respectively. Thus, $\mu_1[0, \frac{1}{2}] = m_0$ and $\mu_1[\frac{1}{2}, 1] = m_1$. In the next steps, every interval is again divided into two subintervals and the mass of the interval is distributed between subintervals in proportion m_0 / m_1. For example, at $k = 2$: $\mu_2[0, \frac{1}{4}]$ $= m_0 m_0$, $\mu_2[\frac{1}{4}, \frac{1}{2}] = \mu_2[\frac{1}{2}, \frac{3}{4}] = m_0 m_1$, $\mu_2[\frac{3}{4}, 1] = m_1 m_1$ and so on. At the kth iteration, mass is partitioned into 2^k intervals of length 2^{-k}. Let us introduce the notion of the binary expansion $0.\beta_1\beta_2 \ldots \beta_k$ for the point $x = \beta_1 2^{-1} + \beta_2 2^{-2} + \beta_k 2^{-k}$ where $0 \le x \le 1$ and $0 < \beta_k < 1$. Then the measure for every dyadic interval $I_{0\beta_1\beta_2 \ldots \beta_k}$ of length 2^{-k} equals

$$\mu_{0\beta_1\beta_2 \ldots \beta_k} = \prod_{i=1}^{k} m_{\beta_i} = m_0{}^n m_1{}^{k-n} \qquad (6.2.3)$$

where n is the number of digits 0 in the address $0\dot{\beta}_1\beta_2 \ldots \beta_k$ of the interval's left end, and (k − n) is the number of digits 1. Since the subinterval mass is preserved at every step, the cascade is called

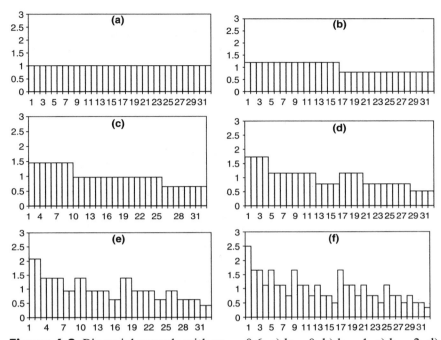

Figure 6.3 Binomial cascade with $m_0 = 0.6$: a) $k = 0$, b) $k = 1$, c) $k = 2$, d) $k = 3$, e) $k = 4$, f) $k = 5$.

conservative or *microcanonical*. The first five steps of the binomial cascade with $m_0 = 0.6$ are depicted in Figure 6.3.

The multifractal spectrum of the binomial cascade equals

$$f(\alpha) = -\frac{\alpha_{max} - \alpha}{\alpha_{max} - \alpha_{min}} \log_2 \left(\frac{\alpha_{max} - \alpha}{\alpha_{max} - \alpha_{min}} \right) - \frac{\alpha - \alpha_{min}}{\alpha_{max} - \alpha_{min}} \log_2 \left(\frac{\alpha - \alpha_{min}}{\alpha_{max} - \alpha_{min}} \right)$$

$$(6.2.4)$$

The distribution (6.2.4) is confined with the interval $[\alpha_{min}, \alpha_{max}]$. If $m_0 \geq 0.5$, then $\alpha_{min} = -\log_2(m_0)$ and $\alpha_{max} = -\log_2(1 - m_0)$. The binomial cascade can be generalized in two directions. First, one can introduce a multinomial cascade by increasing the number of subintervals to $N > 2$. Note that the condition

$$\sum_{0}^{N-1} m_i = 1 \qquad (6.2.5)$$

is needed for preserving the conservative character of the cascade. Secondly, the values of m_i can be randomized rather than assigned fixed values. A cascade with randomized m_i is called *canonical*. In this case, the condition (6.2.5) is satisfied only on average, that is

$$E\left[\sum_0^{N-1} m_i\right] = 1 \qquad (6.2.6)$$

An example of the randomized cascade that has an explicit expression for the multifractal spectrum is the lognormal cascade [6]. In this process, the multiplier that distributes the mass of the interval, M, is determined with the lognormal distribution (i.e., $\log_2(M)$ is drawn from the Gaussian distribution). If the Gaussian mean and variance are λ and σ, respectively, then the conservative character of the cascade $E[M] = 0.5$ is preserved when

$$\sigma^2 = 2(\lambda - 1)/\ln(2) \qquad (6.2.7)$$

The multifractal spectrum of the lognormal cascade that satisfies (6.2.7) equals

$$f(\alpha) = 1 - \frac{(\alpha - \lambda)^2}{4(\lambda - 1)} \qquad (6.2.8)$$

Note that in contrast to the binomial cascade, the lognormal cascade may yield negative values of $f(\alpha)$, which requires interpretation of $f(\alpha)$ other than the fractal dimension.

Innovation of multifractal process, $\Delta X = X(t + \Delta t) - X(t)$, is described with the scaling rule

$$E[|(\Delta X)|^q] = c(q)(\Delta t)^{\tau(q)+1} \qquad (6.2.9)$$

where $c(q)$ and $\tau(q)$ (so-called *scaling function*) are deterministic functions of q. It can be shown that the scaling function $\tau(q)$ is always concave. Obviously, $\tau(0) = -1$. A self-affine process (6.1.4) can be treated as a multifractal process with $\tau(q) = Hq - 1$. In particular, for the Wiener processes, $H = \frac{1}{2}$ and $\tau_w(q) = q/2 - 1$. The scaling function of the binomial cascade can be expressed in terms of its multipliers

$$\tau(q) = \log_2(m_0{}^q + m_1{}^q) \qquad (6.2.10)$$

The scaling function $\tau(q)$ is related to the multifractal spectrum $f(\alpha)$ via the Legendre transformation

$$\tau(q) = \min_{\alpha}[q\alpha - f(\alpha)] \qquad (6.2.11)$$

which is equivalent to

$$f(\alpha) = \arg\min_{q}[q\alpha - \tau(q)] \qquad (6.2.12)$$

Note that $f(\alpha) = q(\alpha - H) + 1$ for the self-affine processes.

In practice, the scaling function of a multifractal process $X(t)$ can be calculated using so-called *partition function*

$$S_q(T, \Delta t) = \sum_{i=0}^{N-1}|X(t + \Delta t) - X(t)|^q \qquad (6.2.13)$$

where the sample $X(t)$ has N points within the interval $[0, T]$ with the mesh size Δt. It follows from (6.2.9) that

$$\log\{E[S_q(T, \Delta t)]\} = \tau(q)\log(\Delta t) + c(q)\log T \qquad (6.2.14)$$

Thus, plotting $\log\{E[S_q(T, \Delta t)]\}$ against $\log(\Delta t)$ for different values of q reveals the character of the scaling function $\tau(q)$. Multifractal models have become very popular in analysis of the financial time series. We shall return to this topic in Section 8.2

6.3 REFERENCES FOR FURTHER READING

The Mandelbrot's work on scaling in the financial time series is compiled in the collection [1]. Among many excellent books on fractals, we choose [2] for its comprehensive material that includes a description of relations between chaos and fractals and an important chapter on multifractals [5].

6.4 EXERCISES

*1. Implement an algorithm that draws the Sierpinski triangle with $\rho = 0.5$ (see Figure 6.2).
   Hint: Choose the following fixed points: (0, 0), (0, 100), (100, 0). Use the following method for the randomized choice of the

fixed point: i = [10 rand( )] %3 where rand( ) is the uniform distribution within [0, 1] and % is modulus (explain the rationale behind this method). Note that at least 10000 iterations are required for a good-quality picture.

*2. Reproduce the first five steps of the binomial cascade with $m_0 = 0.6$ (see Figure 6.3). How will this cascade change if $m_0 = 0.8$?

Chapter 7

Nonlinear Dynamical Systems

7.1 MOTIVATION

It is well known that many nonlinear dynamical systems, including seemingly simple cases, can exhibit chaotic behavior. In short, the presence of chaos implies that very small changes in the initial conditions or parameters of a system can lead to drastic changes in its behavior. In the chaotic regime, the system solutions stay within the phase space region named *strange attractor*. These solutions never repeat themselves; they are not periodic and they never intersect. Thus, in the chaotic regime, the system becomes unpredictable. The chaos theory is an exciting and complex topic. Many excellent books are devoted to the chaos theory and its applications (see, e.g., references in Section 7.7). Here, I only outline the main concepts that may be relevant to quantitative finance.

The first reason to turn to chaotic dynamics is a better understanding of possible causes of price randomness. Obviously, new information coming to the market moves prices. Whether it is a company's performance report, a financial analyst's comments, or a macroeconomic event, the company's stock and option prices may change, thus reflecting the news. Since news usually comes unexpectedly, prices change in unpredictable ways.[1] But is new information the only source reason for price randomness? One may doubt this while observing the price fluctuations at times when no relevant news is released. A tempting proposition is that the price dynamics can be attributed in part to the complexity of financial markets. The possibility that the deterministic processes modulate the price variations has a very important practical implication: even though these processes can have the chaotic regimes, their deterministic nature means that prices may be *partly* forecastable. Therefore, research of chaos in finance and economics is accompanied with discussion of limited predictability of the processes under investigation [1].

There have been several attempts to find possible strange attractors in the financial and economic time series (see, e.g., [1–3] and references therein). Discerning the deterministic chaotic dynamics from a "pure" stochastic process is always a non-trivial task. This problem is even more complicated for financial markets whose parameters may have non-stationary components [4]. So far, there has been little (if any) evidence found of low-dimensional chaos in financial and economic time series. Still, the search of chaotic regimes remains an interesting aspect of empirical research.

There is also another reason for paying attention to the chaotic dynamics. One may introduce chaos inadvertently while modeling financial or economic processes with some nonlinear system. This problem is particularly relevant in agent-based modeling of financial markets where variables generally are not observable (see Chapter 12). Nonlinear continuous systems exhibit possible chaos if their dimension exceeds two. However, nonlinear discrete systems (maps) can become chaotic even in the one-dimensional case. Note that the autoregressive models being widely used in analysis of financial time series (see Section 5.1) are maps in terms of the dynamical systems theory. Thus, a simple nonlinear expansion of a univariate autoregressive map may lead to chaos, while the continuous analog of this model is perfectly predictable. Hence, understanding of nonlinear dynamical effects is important not only for examining empirical time series but also for analyzing possible artifacts of the theoretical modeling.

This chapter continues with a widely popular one-dimensional discrete model, the *logistic map*, which illustrates the major concepts in the chaos theory (Section 7.2). Furthermore, the framework for the continuous systems is introduced in Section 7.3. Then the three-dimensional *Lorenz model*, being the classical example of the low-dimensional continuous chaotic system, is described (Section 7.4). Finally, the main pathways to chaos and the chaos measures are outlined in Section 7.5 and Section 7.6, respectively.

7.2 DISCRETE SYSTEMS: THE LOGISTIC MAP

The logistic map is a simple discrete model that was originally used to describe the dynamics of biological populations (see, e.g., [5] and references therein). Let us consider a variable number of individuals in a population, N. Its value at the k-th time interval is described with the following equation

$$N_k = AN_{k-1} - BN_{k-1}{}^2 \tag{7.2.1}$$

Parameter A characterizes the population growth that is determined by such factors as food supply, climate, etc. Obviously, the population grows only if $A > 1$. If there are no restrictive factors (i.e., when $B = 0$), the growth is exponential, which never happens in nature for long. Finite food supply, predators, and other causes of mortality restrict the population growth, which is reflected in factor B. The maximum value of N_k equals $N^{max} = A/B$. It is convenient to introduce the dimensionless variable $X_k = N_k/N^{max}$. Then $0 \le X_k \le 1$, and equation (7.2.1) has the form

$$X_k = AX_{k-1}(1 - X_{k-1}) \tag{7.2.2}$$

A generic discrete equation in the form

$$X_k = f(X_{k-1}) \tag{7.2.3}$$

is called an *(iterated) map*, and the function $f(X_{k-1})$ is called the *iteration function*. The map (7.2.2) is named the *logistic map*. The sequence of values X_k that are generated by the iteration procedure is called a *trajectory*. Trajectories depend not only on the iteration function but also on the initial value X_0. Some initial points turn out to be the map solution at all iterations. The value X^* that satisfies the equation

$$X^* = f(X^*) \tag{7.2.4}$$

is named the *fixed point* of the map. There are two fixed points for the logistic map (7.2.2):

$$X_1^* = 0, \text{ and } X_2^* = (A - 1)/A \qquad (7.2.5)$$

If $A \leq 1$, the logistic map trajectory approaches the fixed point X_1^* from any initial value $0 \leq X_0 \leq 1$. The set of points that the trajectories tend to approach is called the *attractor*. Generally, nonlinear dynamical systems can have several attractors. The set of initial values from which the trajectories approach a particular attractor are called the *basin of attraction*. For the logistic map with $A < 1$, the attractor is $X_1^* = 0$, and its basin is the interval $0 \leq X_0 \leq 1$.

If $1 < A < 3$, the logistic map trajectories have the attractor $X_2^* = (A - 1)/A$ and its basin is also $0 \leq X_0 \leq 1$. In the mean time, the point $X_1^* = 0$ is the repellent fixed point, which implies that any trajectory that starts near X_1^* tends to move away from it.

A new type of solutions to the logistic map appears at $A > 3$. Consider the case with $A = 3.1$: the trajectory does not have a single attractor but rather oscillates between two values, $X \approx 0.558$ and $X \approx 0.764$. In the biological context, this implies that the growing population overexerts its survival capacity at $X \approx 0.764$. Then the population shrinks "too much" (i.e., to $X \approx 0.558$), which yields capacity for further growth, and so on. This regime is called period-2. The parameter value at which solution changes qualitatively is named the *bifurcation point*. Hence, it is said that the period-doubling bifurcation occurs at $A = 3$. With a further increase of A, the oscillation amplitude grows until A approaches the value of about 3.45. At higher values of A, another period-doubling bifurcation occurs (period-4). This implies that the population oscillates among four states with different capacities for further growth. Period doubling continues with rising A until its value approaches 3.57. Typical trajectories for period-2 and period-8 are given in Figure 7.1. With further growth of A, the number of periods becomes infinite, and the system becomes chaotic. Note that the solution to the logistic map at $A > 4$ is unbounded.

Specifics of the solutions for the logistic map are often illustrated with the bifurcation diagram in which all possible values of X are plotted against A (see Figure 7.2). Interestingly, it seems that there is some order in this diagram even in the chaotic region at $A > 3.6$. This order points to the fractal nature of the chaotic attractor, which will be discussed later on.

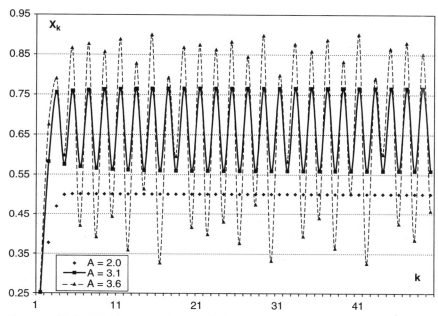

Figure 7.1 Solution to the logistic map at different values of the parameter A.

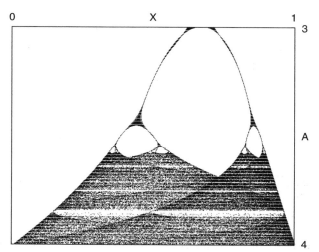

Figure 7.2 The bifurcation diagram of the logistic map in the parameter region $3 \leq A < 4$.

Another manifestation of universality that may be present in chaotic processes is the Feigenbaum's observation of the limiting rate at which the period-doubling bifurcations occur. Namely, if A_n is the value of A at which the period-2^n occurs, then the ratio

$$\delta_n = (A_n - A_{n-1})/(A_{n+1} - A_n) \qquad (7.2.6)$$

has the limit

$$\lim_{n \to \infty} \delta_n = 4.669\ldots \qquad (7.2.7)$$

It turns out that the limit (7.2.7) is valid for the entire family of maps with the parabolic iteration functions [5].

A very important feature of the chaotic regime is extreme sensitivity of trajectories to the initial conditions. This is illustrated with Figure 7.3 for $A = 3.8$. Namely, two trajectories with the initial conditions $X_0 = 0.400$ and $X_0 = 0.405$ diverge completely after 10

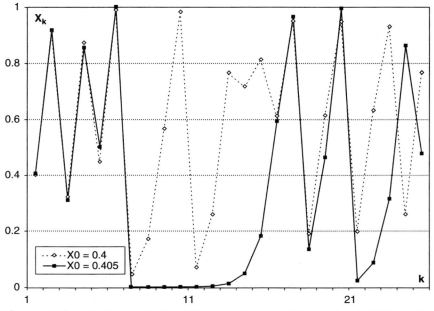

Figure 7.3 Solution to the logistic map for $A = 3.8$ and two initial conditions: $X_0 = 0.400$ and $X_0 = 0.405$.

iterations. Thus, the logistic map provides an illuminating example of complexity and universality generated by interplay of nonlinearity and discreteness.

7.3 CONTINUOUS SYSTEMS

While the discrete time series are the convenient framework for financial data analysis, financial processes are often described using continuous presentation [6]. Hence, we need understanding of the chaos specifics in continuous systems. First, let us introduce several important notions with a simple model of a damped oscillator (see, e.g., [7]). Its equation of motion in terms of the angle of deviation from equilibrium, θ, is

$$\frac{d^2\theta}{dt^2} + \gamma\frac{d\theta}{dt} + \omega^2\theta = 0 \qquad (7.3.1)$$

In (7.3.1), γ is the damping coefficient and ω is the angular frequency. Dynamical systems are often described with *flows*, sets of coupled differential equations of the first order. These equations in the vector notations have the following form

$$\frac{d\mathbf{X}}{dt} = F(\mathbf{X}(t)), \ \mathbf{X} = (X_1, X_2, \ldots X_N)' \qquad (7.3.2)$$

We shall consider so-called *autonomous systems* for which the function F in the right-hand side of (7.3.2) does not depend explicitly on time. A non-autonomous system can be transformed into an autonomous one by treating time in the function $F(\mathbf{X}, t)$ as an additional variable, $X_{N+1} = t$, and adding another equation to the flow

$$\frac{dX_{N+1}}{dt} = 1 \qquad (7.3.3)$$

As a result, the dimension of the phase space increases by one. The notion of the fixed point in continuous systems differs from that of discrete systems (7.2.4). Namely, the fixed points for the flow (7.3.2) are the points $\mathbf{X}^*$ at which all derivatives in its left-hand side equal zero. For the obvious reason, these points are also named the equilibrium (or stationary) points: If the system reaches one of these points, it stays there forever.

Equations with derivatives of order greater than one can be also transformed into flows by introducing additional variables. For example, equation (7.3.1) can be transformed into the system

$$\frac{d\theta}{dt} = \varphi, \quad \frac{d\varphi}{dt} = -\gamma\varphi - \omega^2\theta \qquad (7.3.4)$$

Hence, the damped oscillator may be described in the two-dimensional phase space (φ, θ). The energy of the damped oscillator, E,

$$E = 0.5(\varphi^2 + \omega^2\theta^2) \qquad (7.3.5)$$

evolves with time according to the equation

$$\frac{dE}{dt} = -\gamma\varphi^2 \qquad (7.3.6)$$

It follows from (7.3.6) that the dumped oscillator dissipates energy (i.e., is a *dissipative system*) at $\gamma > 0$. Typical trajectories of the dumped oscillator are shown in Figure 7.4. In the case $\gamma = 0$, the trajectories are circles centered at the origin of the phase plane. If $\gamma > 0$, the trajectories have a form of a spiral approaching the origin of plane.[2] In general, the dissipative systems have a point attractor in the center of coordinates that corresponds to the zero energy.

Chaos is usually associated with dissipative systems. Systems without energy dissipation are named *conservative* or *Hamiltonian*

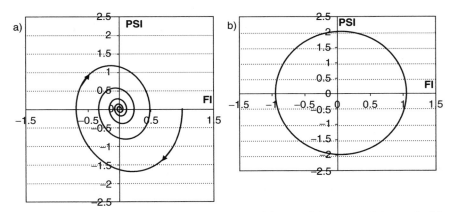

Figure 7.4 Trajectories of the damped oscillator with $\omega = 2$: (a) $\gamma = 2$; (b) $\gamma = 0$.

systems. Some conservative systems may have the chaotic regimes, too (so-called *non-integrable systems*) [5], but this case will not be discussed here. One can easily identify the sources of dissipation in real physical processes, such as friction, heat radiation, and so on. In general, flow (7.3.2) is dissipative if the condition

$$\text{div(F)} \equiv \sum_{i=1}^{N} \frac{\partial F}{\partial X_i} < 0 \qquad (7.3.7)$$

is valid on average within the phase space.

Besides the point attractor, systems with two or more dimensions may have an attractor named the *limit cycle*. An example of such an attractor is the solution of the Van der Pol equation. This equation describes an oscillator with a variable damping coefficient

$$\frac{d^2\theta}{dt^2} + \gamma[(\theta/\theta_0)^2 - 1]\frac{d\theta}{dt} + \omega^2\theta = 0 \qquad (7.3.8)$$

In (7.3.8), θ_0 is a parameter. The damping coefficient is positive at sufficiently high amplitudes $\theta > \theta_0$, which leads to energy dissipation. However, at low amplitudes ($\theta < \theta_0$), the damping coefficient becomes negative. The negative term in (7.3.8) has a sense of an energy source that prevents oscillations from complete decay. If one introduces $\theta_0\sqrt{\omega/\gamma}$ as the unit of amplitude and $1/\omega$ as the unit of time, then equation (7.3.8) acquires the form

$$\frac{d^2\theta}{dt^2} + (\theta^2 - \varepsilon^2)\frac{d\theta}{dt} + \theta = 0 \qquad (7.3.9)$$

where $\varepsilon = \gamma/\omega$ is the only dimensionless parameter that defines the system evolution. The flow describing the Van der Pol equation has the following form

$$\frac{d\theta}{dt} = \varphi, \quad \frac{d\varphi}{dt} = (\varepsilon^2 - \theta^2)\varphi - \theta \qquad (7.3.10)$$

Figure 7.5 illustrates the solution to equation (7.3.1) for $\varepsilon = 0.4$. Namely, the trajectories approach a closed curve from the initial conditions located both outside and inside the limit cycle. It should be noted that the flow trajectories never intersect, even though their graphs may deceptively indicate otherwise. This property follows from uniqueness of solutions to equation (7.3.8). Indeed, if the

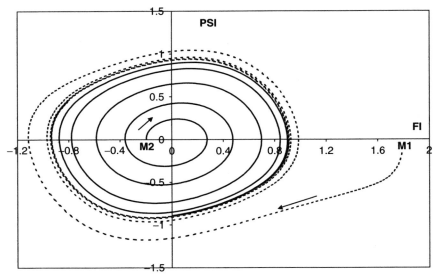

Figure 7.5 Trajectories of the Van der Pol oscillator with $\varepsilon = 0.4$. Both trajectories starting at points M1 and M2, respectively, end up on the same limit circle.

trajectories do intersect, say at point P in the phase space, this implies that the initial condition at point P yields two different solutions.

Since the solution to the Van der Pol equation changes qualitatively from the point attractor to the limit cycle at $\varepsilon = 0$, this point is a bifurcation. Those bifurcations that lead to the limit cycle are named the *Hopf bifurcations*.

In three-dimensional dissipative systems, two new types of attractors appear. First, there are *quasi-periodic attractors*. These trajectories are associated with two different frequencies and are located on the surface of a torus. The following equations describe the toroidal trajectories (see Figure 7.6)

$$x(t) = (R + r\sin(w_r t))\cos(w_R t)$$
$$y(t) = (R + r\sin(w_r t))\sin(w_R t)$$
$$z(t) = r\cos(w_r t) \tag{7.3.11}$$

In (7.3.11), R and r are the external and internal torus radii, respectively; w_R and w_r are the frequencies of rotation around the external

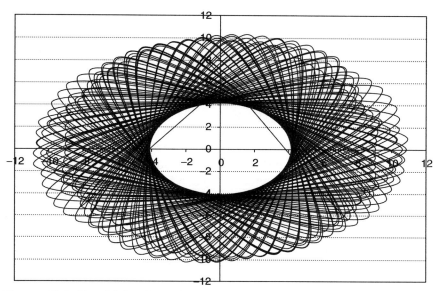

Figure 7.6 Toroidal trajectories (7.3.11) in the X-Y plane for $R = 10$, $r = 1$, $w_R = 100$, $w_r = 3$.

and internal radii, respectively. If the ratio w_R/w_r is irrational, it is said that the frequencies are incommensurate. Then the trajectories (7.3.11) never close on themselves and eventually cover the entire torus surface. Nevertheless, such a motion is predictable, and thus it is not chaotic. Another type of attractor that appears in three-dimensional systems is the strange attractor. It will be introduced using the famous Lorenz model in the next section.

7.4 LORENZ MODEL

The Lorenz model describes the convective dynamics of a fluid layer with three dimensionless variables:

$$\frac{dX}{dt} = p(Y - X)$$
$$\frac{dY}{dt} = -XZ + rX - Y$$
$$\frac{dZ}{dt} = XY - bZ \qquad (7.4.1)$$

In (7.4.1), the variable X characterizes the fluid velocity distribution, and the variables Y and Z describe the fluid temperature distribution. The dimensionless parameters p, r, and b characterize the thermo-hydrodynamic and geometric properties of the fluid layer. The Lorenz model, being independent of the space coordinates, is a result of significant simplifications of the physical process under consideration [5, 7]. Yet, this model exhibits very complex behavior. As it is often done in the literature, we shall discuss the solutions to the Lorenz model for the fixed parameters p = 10 and b = 8/3. The parameter r (which is the vertical temperature difference) will be treated as the control parameter.

At small r ≤ 1, any trajectory with arbitrary initial conditions ends at the state space origin. In other words, the non-convective state at X = Y = Z = 0 is a fixed point attractor and its basin is the entire phase space. At r > 1, the system acquires three fixed points. Hence, the point r = 1 is a bifurcation. The phase space origin is now repellent. Two other fixed points are attractors that correspond to the steady convection with clockwise and counterclockwise rotation, respectively (see Figure 7.7). Note that the initial conditions define

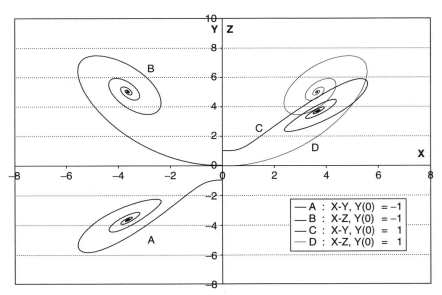

Figure 7.7 Trajectories of the Lorenz model for p = 10, b = 8/3, r = 6, X(0) = Z(0) = 0, and different Y(0).

which of the two attractors is the trajectory's final destination. The locations of the fixed points are determined by the stationary solution

$$\frac{dX}{dt} = \frac{dY}{dt} = \frac{dZ}{dt} = 0 \qquad (7.4.2)$$

Namely,

$$Y = X, \ Z = 0.5X^2, \ X = \pm\sqrt{b(r-1)} \qquad (7.4.3)$$

When the parameter r increases to about 13.93, the repelling regions develop around attractors. With further growth of r, the trajectories acquire the famous "butterfly" look (see Figure 7.8). In this region, the system becomes extremely sensitive to initial conditions. An example with r = 28 in Figure 7.9 shows that the change of Y(0) in 1% leads to completely different trajectories Y(t). The system is then unpredictable, and it is said that its attractors are "strange."

With further growth of the parameter r, the Lorenz model reveals new surprises. Namely, it has "windows of periodicity" where the trajectories may be chaotic at first but then become periodic. One of the largest among such windows is in the range 144 < r < 165. In this parameter region, the oscillation period decreases when r grows. Note

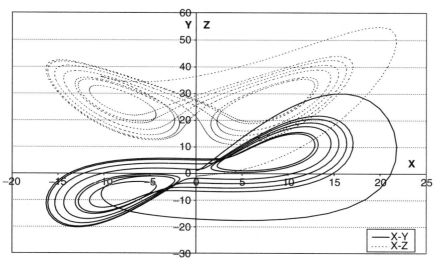

Figure 7.8 Trajectories of the Lorenz model for p = 10, b = 8/3 and r = 28.

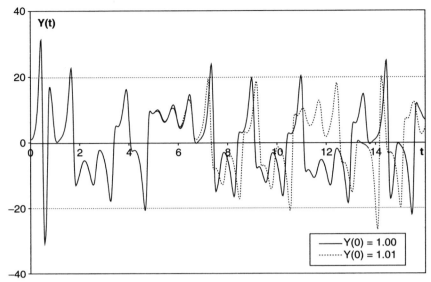

Figure 7.9 Sensitivity of the Lorenz model to the initial conditions for p = 10, b = 8/3 and r = 28.

that this periodicity is not described with a single frequency, and the maximums of its peaks vary. Finally, at very high values of r (r > 313), the system acquires a single stable limit cycle. This fascinating manifold of solutions is not an exclusive feature of the Lorenz model. Many nonlinear dissipative systems exhibit a wide spectrum of solutions including chaotic regimes.

7.5 PATHWAYS TO CHAOS

A number of general pathways to chaos in nonlinear dissipative systems have been described in the literature (see, e.g., [5] and references therein). All transitions to chaos can be divided into two major groups: *local bifurcations* and *global bifurcations*. Local bifurcations occur in some parameter range, but the trajectories become chaotic when the system control parameter reaches the critical value. Three types of local bifurcations are discerned: period-doubling, quasi-periodicity, and intermittency. *Period-doubling* starts with a limit cycle at some value of the system control parameter. With further change of this parameter, the trajectory period doubles and doubles until it becomes infinite. This process was proposed by Landau as the main turbulence mechanism. Namely, laminar flow develops oscillations at some sufficiently high velocity. As velocity increases, another (incommensurate) frequency appears in the flow, and so on. Finally, the frequency spectrum has the form of a practically continuous band. An alternative mechanism of turbulence (*quasi-periodicity*) was proposed by Ruelle and Takens. They have shown that the quasi-periodic trajectories confined on the torus surface can become chaotic due to high sensitivity to the input parameters. *Intermittency* is a broad category itself. Its pathway to chaos consists of a sequence of periodic and chaotic regions. With changing the control parameter, chaotic regions become larger and larger and eventually fill the entire space.

In the global bifurcations, the trajectories approach simple attractors within some control parameter range. With further change of the control parameter, these trajectories become increasingly complicated and in the end, exhibit chaotic motion. Global bifurcations are partitioned into crises and chaotic transients. *Crises* include sudden changes in the size of chaotic attractors, sudden appearances of the chaotic attractors, and sudden destructions of chaotic attractors and their basins. In *chaotic transients*, typical trajectories initially behave in an apparently chaotic manner for some time, but then move to some other region of the phase space. This movement may asymptotically approach a non-chaotic attractor.

Unfortunately, there is no simple rule for determining the conditions at which chaos appears in a given flow. Moreover, the same system may become chaotic in different ways depending on its parameters. Hence, attentive analysis is needed for every particular system.

7.6 MEASURING CHAOS

As it was noticed in in Section 7.1, it is important to understand whether randomness of an empirical time series is caused by noise or by the chaotic nature of the underlying deterministic process. To address this problem, let us introduce the *Lyapunov exponent*. The major property of a chaotic attractor is exponential divergence of its nearby trajectories. Namely, if two nearby trajectories are separated by distance d_0 at $t = 0$, the separation evolves as

$$d(t) = d_0 \exp(\lambda t) \tag{7.6.1}$$

The parameter λ in (7.6.1) is called the Lyapunov exponent. For the rigorous definition, consider two points in the phase space, X_0 and $X_0 + \Delta x_0$, that generate two trajectories with some flow (7.3.2). If the function $\Delta x(X_0, t)$ defines evolution of the distance between these points, then

$$\lambda = \lim \frac{1}{t} \ln \frac{|\Delta x(X_0, t)|}{|\Delta x_0|}, \; t \to \infty, \; \Delta x_0 \to 0 \tag{7.6.2}$$

When $\lambda < 0$, the system is asymptotically stable. If $\lambda = 0$, the system is conservative. Finally, the case with $\lambda > 0$ indicates chaos since the system trajectories diverge exponentially.

The practical receipt for calculating the Lyapunov exponent is as follows. Consider n observations of a time series $x(t)$: $x(t_k) = x_k$, $k = 1$, ..., n. First, select a point x_i and another point x_j close to x_i. Then calculate the distances

$$d_0 = |x_i - x_j|, \; d_1 = |x_{i+1} - x_{j+1}|, \ldots, d_n = |x_{i+n} - x_{j+n}| \tag{7.6.3}$$

If the distance between x_{i+n} and x_{j+n} evolves with n accordingly with (7.6.1), then

$$\lambda(x_i) = \frac{1}{n} \ln \frac{d_n}{d_0} \tag{7.6.4}$$

The value of the Lyapunov exponent $\lambda(x_i)$ in (7.6.4) is expected to be sensitive to the choice of the initial point x_i. Therefore, the average value over a large number of trials N of $\lambda(x_i)$ is used in practice

$$\lambda = \frac{1}{N} \sum_{i=1}^{N} \lambda(x_i) \tag{7.6.5}$$

Due to the finite size of empirical data samples, there are limitations on the values of n and N, which affects the accuracy of calculating the Lyapunov exponent. More details about this problem, as well as other chaos quantifiers, such as the Kolmogorov-Sinai entropy, can be found in [5] and references therein.

The generic characteristic of the strange attractor is its fractal dimension. In fact, the non-integer (i.e., fractal) dimension of an attractor can be used as the definition of a strange attractor. In Chapter 6, the box-counting fractal dimension was introduced. A computationally simpler alternative, so-called *correlation dimension*, is often used in nonlinear dynamics [3, 5].

Consider a sample with N trajectory points within an attractor. To define the correlation dimension, first the relative number of points located within the distance R from the point i must be calculated

$$p_i(R) = \frac{1}{N-1} \sum_{j=1, j \neq i}^{N} \theta(R - |x_j - x_i|) \qquad (7.6.6)$$

In (7.6.6), the Heaviside step function θ equals

$$\theta = \begin{cases} 0, & x < 0 \\ 1, & x \geq 0 \end{cases} \qquad (7.6.7)$$

Then the correlation sum that characterizes the probability of finding two trajectory points within the distance R is computed

$$C(R) = \frac{1}{N} \sum_{i=1}^{N} p_i(R) \qquad (7.6.8)$$

It is assumed that $C(R) \sim R^{D_c}$. Hence, the correlation dimension D_c equals

$$D_c = \lim_{R \to 0} \left[\ln C(R) / \ln R \right] \qquad (7.6.9)$$

There is an obvious problem of finding the limit (7.6.9) for data samples on a finite grid. Yet, plotting $\ln[C(R)]$ versus $\ln(R)$ (which is expected to yield a linear graph) provides an estimate of the correlation dimension.

An interesting question is whether a strange attractor is always chaotic, in other words, if it always has a positive Lyapunov exponent. It turns out there are rare situations when an attractor may be strange but not chaotic. One such example is the logistic map at the period-doubling points: Its Lyapunov exponent equals zero while the fractal dimension is about 0.5. Current opinion, however, holds that the strange deterministic attractors may appear in discrete maps rather than in continuous systems [5].

7.7 REFERENCES FOR FURTHER READING

Two popular books, the journalistic report by Gleick [8] and the "first-hand" account by Ruelle [9], offer insight into the science of chaos and the people behind it. The textbook by Hilborn [5] provides a comprehensive description of the subject. The interrelations between the chaos theory and fractals are discussed in detail in [10].

7.8 EXERCISES

1. Consider the quadratic map $X_k = X_{k-1}^2 + C$, where $C > 0$.
   (a) Prove that $C = 0.25$ is a bifurcation point.
   (b) Find fixed points for $C = 0.125$. Define what point is an attractor and what is its attraction basin for $X > 0$.
2. Verify the equilibrium points of the Lorenz model (7.4.3).
*3. Calculate the Lyapunov exponent of the logistic map as a function of the parameter A.
*4. Implement the algorithm for simulating the Lorenz model.
   (a) Reproduce the "butterfly" trajectories depicted in Figure 7.8.
   (b) Verify existence of the periodicity window at $r = 150$.
   (c) Verify existence of the limit cycle at $r = 350$.
   Hint: *Use a simple algorithm:* $X_k = X_{k-1} + \tau F(X_{k-1}, Y_{k-1}, Z_{k-1})$ *where the time step τ can be assigned 0.01.*

Chapter 8

Scaling in Financial Time Series

8.1 INTRODUCTION

Two well-documented findings motivate further analysis of financial time series. First, the probability distributions of returns often deviate significantly from the normal distribution by having fat tails and excess kurtosis. Secondly, returns exhibit volatility clustering. The latter effect has led to the development of the GARCH models described in Section 5.3.[1] In this chapter, we shall focus on scaling in the probability distributions of returns, the concept that has attracted significant attention from economists and physicists alike.

Alas, as the leading experts in Econophysics, H. E. Stanley and R. Mantegna acknowledged [2]:

> "No model exists for the stochastic process describing the time evolution of the logarithm of price that is accepted by all researchers."

There are several reasons for the status quo.[2] First, different financial time series may have varying non-stationary components. Indeed, the stock price reflects not only the current value of a company's assets but also the expectations of the company's growth. Yet, there is no general pattern for evolution of a business enterprise.[3] Therefore, empirical research often concentrates on the average economic indexes, such as the S&P 500. Averaging over a large number of companies certainly smoothes noise. Yet, the composition of these indicators is dynamic: Companies may be added to or dropped from indexes, and the company's contribution to the economic index usually depends on its ever-changing market capitalization.

Foreign exchange rates are another object frequently used in empirical research.[4] Unfortunately, many of the findings accumulated during the 1990s have become somewhat irrelevant, as several European currencies ceased to exist after the birth of the Euro in 1999. In any case, the foreign exchange rates, being a measure of relative currency strength, may have statistical features that differ among themselves and in comparison with the economic indicators of single countries.

Another problem is data granularity. Low granularity may underestimate the contributions of market rallies and crashes. On the other hand, high-frequency data are extremely noisy. Hence, one may expect that universal properties of financial time series (if any exist) have both short-range and long-range time limitations.

The current theoretical framework might be too simplistic to accurately describe the real world. Yet, important advances in understanding of scaling in finance have been made in recent years. In the next section, the asymptotic power laws that may be recovered from the financial time series are discussed. In Section 8.3, the recent developments including the multifractal approach are outlined.

8.2 POWER LAWS IN FINANCIAL DATA

The importance of long-range dependencies in the financial time series was shown first by B. Mandelbrot [6]. Using the R/S analysis (see Section 6.1), Mandelbrot and others have found multiple deviations of the empirical probability distributions from the normal distribution [7].

Early research of universality in the financial time series [6] was based on the stable distributions (see Section 3.3). This approach, however, has fallen out of favor because the stable distributions have infinite volatility, which is unacceptable for many financial applications [8]. The truncated Levy flights that satisfy the requirement for finite volatility have been used as a way around this problem [2, 9, 10]. One disadvantage of the truncated Levy flights is that the truncating distance yields an additional fitting parameter. More importantly, the recent research by H. Stanley and others indicates that the asymptotic probability distributions of several typical financial time series resemble the power law with the index α close to three [11–13]. This means that the probability distributions examined by Stanley's team are not stable at all (recall that the stable distributions satisfy the condition $0 < \alpha \leq 2$). Let us provide more details about these interesting findings.

In [11], returns of the S&P 500 index were studied for the period 1984–1996 with the time scales Δt varying from 1 minute to 1 month. It was found that the probability distributions at $\Delta t < 4$ days were consistent with the power-law asymptotic behavior with the index $\alpha \approx 3$. At $\Delta t > 4$ days, the distributions slowly converge to the normal distribution. Similar results were obtained for daily returns of the NIKKEI index and the Hang-Seng index. These results are complemented by another work [12] where the returns of several thousand U.S. companies were analyzed for Δt in the range from five minutes to about four years. It was found that the returns of individual companies at $\Delta t < 16$ days are also described with the power-law distribution having the index $\alpha \approx 3$. At longer Δt, the probability distributions slowly approach the normal form. It was also shown that the probability distributions of the S&P 500 index and of individual companies have the same asymptotic behavior due to the strong cross-correlations of the companies' returns. When these cross-correlations were destroyed with randomization of the time series, the probability distributions converged to normal at a much faster pace.

The theoretical model offered in [13] may provide some explanation to the power-law distribution of returns with the index $\alpha \approx 3$. This model is based on two observations: (a) the distribution of the trading volumes obeys the power law with an index of about 1.5; and (b) the distribution of the number of trades is a power law with an index of about three (in fact, it is close to 3.4). Two assumptions were made to derive the index α of three. First, it was assumed that the price movements were caused primarily by the activity of large mutual funds whose size distribution is the power law with index of one (so-called Zipf's law [4]). In addition, it was assumed that the mutual fund managers trade in an optimal way.

Another model that generates the power law distributions is the stochastic *Lotka-Volterra system* (see [14] and references therein). The generic Lotka-Volterra system is used for describing different phenomena, particularly the population dynamics with the predator-prey interactions. For our discussion, it is important that some agent-based models of financial markets (see Chapter 12) can be reduced to the Lotka-Volterra system [15]. The discrete Lotka-Volterra system has the form

$$w_i(t+1) = \lambda(t)w_i(t) - aW(t) - bw_i(t)W(t), \quad W(t) = \frac{1}{N}\sum_{i=1}^{N} w_i(t) \quad (8.2.1)$$

where w_i is an individual characteristic (e.g., wealth of an investor i; $i = 1, 2, \ldots, N$), a and b are the model parameters, and $\lambda(t)$ is a random variable. The components of this system evolve spontaneously into the power law distribution $f(w, t) \sim w^{-(1+\alpha)}$. In the mean time, evolution of $W(t)$ exhibits intermittent fluctuations that can be parameterized using the truncated Levy distribution with the same index α [14].

Seeking universal properties of the financial market crashes is another interesting problem explored by Sornette and others (see [16] for details). The main idea here is that financial crashes are caused by collective trader behavior (dumping stocks in panic), which resembles the critical phenomena in hierarchical systems. Within this analogy, the asymptotic behavior of the asset price $S(t)$ has the log-periodic form

$$S(t) = A + B(t_c - t)^\alpha \{1 + C\cos[w\ln(t_c - t) - \varphi]\} \quad (8.2.2)$$

where t_c is the crash time; A, B, C, w, α, and φ are the fitting parameters. There has been some success in describing several market crashes with the log-periodic asymptotes [16]. Criticism of this approach is given in [17] and references therein.

8.3 NEW DEVELOPMENTS

So, do the findings listed in the preceding section solve the problem of scaling in finance? This remains to be seen. First, B. LeBaron has shown how the price distributions that seem to have the power-law form can be generated by a mix of the normal distributions with different time scales [18]. In this work, the daily returns are assumed to have the form

$$R(t) = \exp[\gamma x(t) + \mu]\varepsilon(t) \tag{8.3.1}$$

where $\varepsilon(t)$ is an independent random normal variable with zero mean and unit variance. The function $x(t)$ is the sum of three processes with different characteristic times

$$x(t) = a_1 y_1(t) + a_2 y_2(t) + a_3 y_3(t) \tag{8.3.2}$$

The first process $y_1(t)$ is an AR(1) process

$$y_1(t+1) = \rho_1 y_1(t) + \eta_1(t+1) \tag{8.3.3}$$

where $\rho_1 = 0.999$ and $\eta_1(t)$ is an independent Gaussian adjusted so that $\text{var}[y_1(t)] = 1$. While AR(1) yields exponential decay, the chosen value of ρ_1 gives a long-range half-life of about 2.7 years. Similarly,

$$y_2(t+1) = \rho_2 y_2(t) + \eta_2(t+1) \tag{8.3.4}$$

where $\eta_2(t)$ is an independent Gaussian adjusted so that $\text{var}[y_2(t)] = 1$. The chosen value $\rho_2 = 0.95$ gives a half-life of about 2.5 weeks. The process $y_3(t)$ is an independent Gaussian with unit variance and zero mean, which retains volatility shock for one day. The normalization rule is applied to the coefficients a_i

$$a_1{}^2 + a_2{}^2 + a_3{}^2 = 1. \tag{8.3.5}$$

The parameters a_1, a_2, γ, and μ are chosen to adjust the empirical data. This model was used for analysis of the Dow returns for 100 years (from 1900 to 2000). The surprising outcome of this analysis is retrieval of the power law with the index in the range of 2.98 to 3.33 for the data aggregation ranges of 1 to 20 days. Then there are generic comments by T. Lux on spurious scaling laws that may be extracted from finite financial data samples [19]. Some reservation has also been expressed about the graphical inference method widely used in the empirical research. In this method, the linear regression equations are recovered from the log - log plots. While such an approach may provide correct asymptotes, at times it does not stand up to more rigorous statistical hypothesis testing. A case in point is the distribution in the form

$$f(x) = x^{-\alpha} L(x) \tag{8.3.6}$$

where $L(x)$ is a slowly-varying function that determines behavior of the distribution in the short-range region. Obviously, the "universal" scaling exponent $\alpha = -\log[f(x)]/\log(x)$ is as accurate as $L(x)$ is close to a constant. This problem is relevant also to the multifractal scaling analysis that has become another "hot" direction in the field.

The multifractal patterns have been found in several financial time series (see, e.g., [20, 21] and references therein). The multifractal framework has been further advanced by Mandelbrot and others. They proposed *compound stochastic process* in which a multifractal cascade is used for time transformations [22]. Namely, it was assumed that the price returns $R(t)$ are described as

$$R(t) = B_H[\theta(t)] \qquad (8.3.7)$$

where $B_H[]$ is the fractional Brownian motion with index H and $\theta(t)$ is a distribution function of multifractal measure (see Section 6.2). Both stochastic components of the compound process are assumed independent. The function $\theta(t)$ has a sense of "trading time" that reflects intensity of the trading process. Current research in this direction shows some promising results [23–26]. In particular, it was shown that both the binomial cascade and the lognormal cascade embedded into the Wiener process (i.e., into $B_H[]$ with $H = 0.5$) may yield a more accurate description of several financial time series than the GARCH model [23]. Nevertheless, this chapter remains "unfinished" as new findings in empirical research continue to pose new challenges for theoreticians.

8.4 REFERENCES FOR FURTHER READING

Early research of scaling in finance is described in [2, 6, 7, 9, 17]. For recent findings in this field, readers may consult [10–13, 23–26].

8.5 EXERCISES

**1. Verify how a sum of Gaussians can reproduce a distribution with the power-law tails in the spirit of [18].

**2. Discuss the recent polemics on the power-law tails of stock prices [27–29].

**3. Discuss the scaling properties of financial time series reported in [30].

Chapter 9

Option Pricing

This chapter begins with an introduction of the notion of financial derivative in Section 9.1. The general properties of the stock options are described in Section 9.2. Furthermore, the option pricing theory is presented using two approaches: the method of the binomial trees (Section 9.3) and the classical Black-Scholes theory (Section 9.4). A paradox related to the arbitrage free portfolio paradigm on which the Black-Scholes theory is based is described in the Appendix section.

9.1 FINANCIAL DERIVATIVES

In finance, *derivatives*[1] are the instruments whose price depends on the value of another (underlying) asset [1]. In particular, the stock option is a derivative whose price depends on the underlying stock price. Derivatives have also been used for many other assets, including but not limited to commodities (e.g., cattle, lumber, copper), Treasury bonds, and currencies.

An example of a simple derivative is a *forward contract* that obliges its owner to buy or sell a certain amount of the underlying asset at a specified price (so-called forward price or delivery price) on a specified date (delivery date or *maturity*). The party involved in a contract as a buyer is said to have a *long position*, while a seller is said to have a *short position*. A forward contract is settled at maturity when the seller delivers the asset to the buyer and the buyer pays the cash amount at the delivery price. At maturity, the current (*spot*) asset price, S_T, may differ from the delivery price, K. Then the payoff from the long position is $S_T - K$ and the payoff from the short position is $K - S_T$.

Future contracts are the forward contracts that are traded on organized exchanges, such as the Chicago Board of Trade (CBOT) and the Chicago Mercantile Exchange (CME). The exchanges determine the standardized amounts of traded assets, delivery dates, and the transaction protocols.

In contrast to the forward and future contracts, *options* give an option holder the right to trade an underlying asset rather than the obligation to do this. In particular, the *call option* gives its holder the right to buy the underlying asset at a specific price (so-called *exercise price* or *strike price*) by a certain date (*expiration date* or maturity). The *put option* gives its holder the right to sell the underlying asset at a strike price by an expiration date. Two basic option types are the European options and the American options.[2] The European options can be exercised only on the expiration date while the American options can be exercised any time up to the expiration date. Most of the current trading options are American. Yet, it is often easier to analyze the European options and use the results for deriving properties of the corresponding American options.

The option pricing theory has been an object of intensive research since the pioneering works of Black, Merton, and Scholes in the 1970s. Still, as we shall see, it poses many challenges.

9.2 GENERAL PROPERTIES OF STOCK OPTIONS

The stock option price is determined with six factors:

- Current stock price, S
- Strike price, K
- Time to maturity, T
- Stock price volatility, σ
- Risk-free interest rate,[3] r
- Dividends paid during the life of the option, D.

Let us discuss how each of these factors affects the option price providing all other factors are fixed. Longer maturity time increases the value of an American option since its holders have more time to exercise it with profit. Note that this is not true for a European option that can be exercised only at maturity date. All other factors, however, affect the American and European options in similar ways.

The effects of the stock price and the strike price are opposite for call options and put options. Namely, payoff of a call option increases while payoff of a put option decreases with rising difference between the stock price and the strike price.

Growing volatility increases the value of both call options and put options: it yields better chances to exercise them with higher payoff. In the mean time, potential losses cannot exceed the option price.

The effect of the risk-free rate is not straightforward. At a fixed stock price, the rising risk-free rate increases the value of the call option. Indeed, the option holder may defer paying for shares and invest this payment into the risk-free assets until the option matures. On the contrary, the value of the put option decreases with the risk-free rate since the option holder defers receiving payment from selling shares and therefore cannot invest them into the risk-free assets. However, rising interest rates often lead to falling stock prices, which may change the resulting effect of the risk-free rate.

Dividends effectively reduce the stock prices. Therefore, dividends decrease value of call options and increase value of put options.

Now, let us consider the payoffs at maturity for four possible European option positions. The *long call option* means that the investor buys the right to buy an underlying asset. Obviously, it makes sense to exercise the option only if $S > K$. Therefore, its payoff is

$$P_{LC} = \max [S - K, 0] \qquad (9.2.1)$$

The *short call option* means that the investor sells the right to buy an underlying asset. This option is exercised if $S > K$, and its payoff is

$$P_{SC} = \min [K - S, 0] \qquad (9.2.2)$$

The *long put option* means that the investor buys the right to sell an underlying asset. This option is exercised when $K > S$, and its payoff is

$$P_{LP} = \max [K - S, 0] \qquad (9.2.3)$$

The *short put option* means that the investor sells the right to sell an underlying asset. This option is exercised when $K > S$, and its payoff is

$$P_{SP} = \min[S - K, 0] \qquad (9.2.4)$$

Note that the option payoff by definition does not account for the option price (also named *option premium*). In fact, option writers sell options at a premium while option buyers pay this premium. Therefore, the option seller's profit is the option payoff plus the option price, while the option buyer's profit is the option payoff minus the option price (see examples in Figure 9.1).

The European call and put options with the same strike price satisfy the relation called *put-call parity*. Consider two portfolios. Portfolio I has one European call option at price c with the strike price K and amount of cash (or zero-coupon bond) with the present value $Kexp[-r(T - t)]$. Portfolio II has one European put option at price p and one share at price S. First, let us assume that share does not pay dividends. Both portfolios at maturity have the same value: $\max(S_T, K)$. Hence,

$$c + Kexp[-r(T - t)] = p + S \qquad (9.2.5)$$

Dividends affect the put-call parity. Namely, the dividends D being paid during the option lifetime have the same effect as the cash future value. Thus,

$$c + D + K\exp[-r(T - t)] = p + S \qquad (9.2.6)$$

Because the American options may be exercised before maturity, the relations between the American put and call prices can be derived only in the form of inequalities [1].

Options are widely used for both speculation and risk hedging. Consider two examples with the IBM stock options. At market closing on 7-Jul-03, the IBM stock price was $83.95. The (American) call option price at maturity on 3-Aug-03 was $2.55 for the strike price of $85. Hence, the buyer of this option at market closing on 7-Jul-03 assumed that the IBM stock price would exceed $(85 + 2.55) = $87.55 before or on 3-Aug-03. If the IBM share price would reach say $90, the option buyer will exercise the call option to buy the share for $85 and immediately sell it for $90. The resulting profit[4] is $(90-87.55) = $2.45. Thus, the return on exercising this option equals 2.45/2.55*100% = 96%. Note that the return on buying an IBM share in this case would only be (90 − 83.95)/83.95*100% = 7.2%.

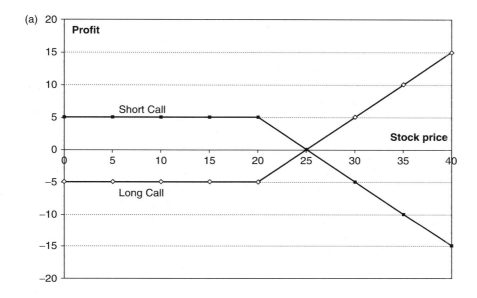

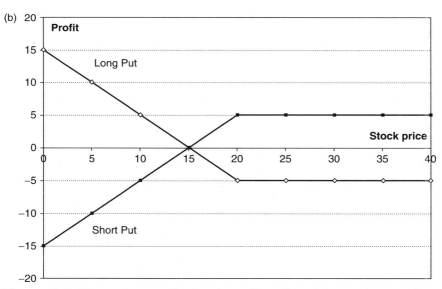

Figure 9.1 The option profits for the strike price of $25 and the option premium of $5: (a) calls, (b) puts.

If, however, the IBM share price stays put through 3-Aug-03, an option buyer incurs losses of $2.45 (i.e., 100%). In the mean time, a share buyer has no losses and may continue to hold shares, hoping that their price will grow in future.

At market closing on 7-Jul-03, the put option for the IBM share with the strike price of $80 at maturity on 3-Aug-03 was $1.50. Hence, buyers of this put option bet on price falling below $(80−1.50) = $78.50. If, say the IBM stock price falls to $75, the buyer of the put option has a gain of $(78.50 − 75) = $3.50.

Now, consider hedging in which the investor buys simultaneously one share for $83.95 and a put option with the strike price of $80 for $1.50. The investor has gains only if the stock price rises above $(83.95 + 1.50) =$85.45. However, if the stock price falls to say $75, the investor's loss is $(80 − 85.45) = −$5.45 rather than the loss of $(75 − 83.95) = −$8.95 incurred without hedging with the put option. Hence, in the given example, the hedging expense of $1.50 allows the investor to save $(−5.45 + 8.95) =$3.40.

9.3 BINOMIAL TREES

Let us consider a simple yet instructive method for option pricing that employs a discrete model called the *binomial tree*. This model is based on the assumption that the current stock price S can change at the next moment only to either the higher value Su or the lower value Sd (where $u > 1$ and $d < 1$). Let us start with the first step of the binomial tree (see Figure 9.2). Let the current option price be equal to F and denote it with F_u or F_d at the next moment when the stock price moves up or down, respectively. Consider now a portfolio that consists of Δ long shares and one short option. This portfolio is risk-free if its value does not depend on whether the stock price moves up or down, that is,

$$Su\Delta - F_u = Sd\Delta - F_d \qquad (9.3.1)$$

Then the number of shares in this portfolio equals

$$\Delta = (F_u - F_d)/(Su - Sd) \qquad (9.3.2)$$

The risk-free portfolio with the current value $(S\Delta - F)$ has the future value $(Su\Delta - F_u) = (Sd\Delta - F_d)$. If the time interval is τ and the risk-

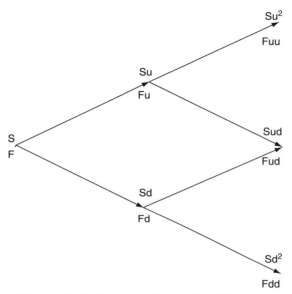

Figure 9.2 Two-step binomial pricing tree.

free interest rate is r, the relation between the portfolio's present value and future value is

$$(S\Delta - F)\exp(r\tau) = Su\Delta - F_u \qquad (9.3.3)$$

Combining (9.3.2) and (9.3.3) yields

$$F = \exp(-r\tau)[pF_u + (1 - p)F_d] \qquad (9.3.4)$$

where

$$p = [\exp(r\tau) - d]/(u - d) \qquad (9.3.5)$$

The factors p and $(1 - p)$ in (9.3.4) have the sense of the probabilities for the stock price to move up and down, respectively. Then, the expectation of the stock price at time τ is

$$E[S(\tau)] = E[pSu + (1 - p)Sd] = S\exp(r\tau) \qquad (9.3.6)$$

This means that the stock price grows on average with the risk-free rate. The framework within which the assets grow with the risk-free rate is called *risk-neutral valuation*. It can be discussed also in terms of the arbitrage theorem [4]. Indeed, violation of the equality (9.3.3) implies that the arbitrage opportunity exists for the portfolio. For example, if the left-hand side of (9.3.3) is greater than its right-hand side, one can immediately make a profit by selling the portfolio and buying the risk-free asset.

Let us proceed to the second step of the binomial tree. Using equation (9.3.4), we receive the following relations between the option prices on the first and second steps

$$F_u = \exp(-r\tau)[pF_{uu} + (1 - p)F_{ud}] \qquad (9.3.7)$$

$$F_d = \exp(-r\tau)[pF_{ud} + (1 - p)F_{dd}] \qquad (9.3.8)$$

The combination of (9.3.4) with (9.3.7) and (9.3.8) yields the current option price in terms of the option prices at the next step

$$F = \exp(-2r\tau)[p^2F_{uu} + 2p(1 - p)F_{ud} + (1 - p)^2F_{dd}] \qquad (9.3.9)$$

This approach can be generalized for a tree with an arbitrary number of steps. Namely, first the stock prices at every node are calculated by going forward from the first node to the final nodes. When the stock prices at the final nodes are known, we can determine the option prices at the final nodes by using the relevant payoff relation (e.g., (9.2.1) for the long call option). Then we calculate the option prices at all other nodes by going backward from the final nodes to the first node and using the recurrent relations similar to (9.3.7) and (9.3.8).

The factors that determine the price change, u and d, can be estimated from the known stock price volatility [1]. In particular, it is generally assumed that prices follow the geometric Brownian motion

$$dS = \mu Sdt + \sigma SdW \qquad (9.3.10)$$

where μ and σ are the drift and diffusion parameters, respectively, and dW is the standard Wiener process (see Section 4.2). Hence, the price changes within the time interval [0, t] are described with the lognormal distribution

$$\ln S(t) = N(\ln S_0 + (\mu - \sigma^2/2)t, \ \sigma\sqrt{t}) \qquad (9.3.11)$$

In (9.3.11), $S_0 = S(0)$, $N(m, \sigma)$ is the normal distribution with mean m and standard deviation σ. It follows from equation (9.3.11) that the expectation of the stock price and its variance at time t equal

$$E[S(t)] = S_0 \exp(\mu t) \qquad (9.3.12)$$

$$\text{Var}[S(t)] = S_0^2 \exp(2\mu t)[\exp(\sigma^2 t) - 1] \qquad (9.3.13)$$

In addition, equation (9.3.6) yields

$$\exp(rt) = pu + (1 - p)d \qquad (9.3.14)$$

Using (9.3.13) and (9.3.14) in the equality $(y) = E[y^2] - E[y]^2$, we obtain the relation

$$\exp(2rt + \sigma^2 t) = pu^2 + (1 - p)d^2 \qquad (9.3.15)$$

The equations (9.3.14) and (9.3.15) do not suffice to define the three parameters d, p, and u. Usually, the additional condition

$$u = 1/d \qquad (9.3.16)$$

is employed. When the time interval Δt is small, the linear approximation to the system of equations (9.3.14) through (9.3.16) yields

$$p = [\exp(r\Delta t) - d]/(u - d), \ u = 1/d = \exp[\sigma(\Delta t)^{1/2}] \qquad (9.3.17)$$

The binomial tree model can be generalized in several ways [1]. In particular, dividends and variable interest rates can be included. The trinomial tree model can also be considered. In the latter model, the stock price may move upward or downward, or it may stay the same. The drawback of the discrete tree models is that they allow only for predetermined innovations of the stock price. Moreover, as it was described above, the continuous model of the stock price dynamics (9.3.10) is used to estimate these innovations. It seems natural then to derive the option pricing theory completely within the continuous framework.

9.4 BLACK-SCHOLES THEORY

The basic assumptions of the classical option pricing theory are that the option price F(t) at time t is a continuous function of time and its underlying asset's price S(t)

$$F = F(S(t), t) \qquad (9.4.1)$$

and that price S(t) follows the geometric Brownian motion (9.3.10) [5, 6]. Several other assumptions are made to simplify the derivation of the final results. In particular,

- There are no market imperfections, such as price discreteness, transaction costs, taxes, and trading restrictions including those on short selling.
- Unlimited risk-free borrowing is available at a constant rate, r.
- There are no arbitrage opportunities.
- There are no dividend payments during the life of the option.

Now, let us derive the classical *Black-Scholes equation*. Since it is assumed that the option price F(t) is described with equation (9.4.1) and price of the underlying asset follows equation (9.3.10), we can use the Ito's expression (4.3.5)

$$dF(S, t) = \left[\mu S \frac{\partial F}{\partial S} + \frac{\partial F}{\partial t} + \frac{\sigma^2}{2} S^2 \frac{\partial^2 F}{\partial S^2}\right] dt + \sigma S \frac{\partial F}{\partial S} dW(t) \qquad (9.4.2)$$

Furthermore, we build a portfolio P with eliminated random contribution dW. Namely, we choose -1 (short) option and $\frac{\partial F}{\partial S}$ shares of the underlying asset,[5]

$$P = -F + \frac{\partial F}{\partial S} S \qquad (9.4.3)$$

The change of the value of this portfolio within the time interval dt equals

$$dP = -dF + \frac{\partial F}{\partial S} dS \qquad (9.4.4)$$

Since there are no arbitrage opportunities, this change must be equal to the interest earned by the portfolio value invested in the risk-free asset

$$dP = rP\, dt \qquad (9.4.5)$$

The combination of equations (9.4.2)–(9.4.5) yields the Black-Scholes equation

$$\frac{\partial F}{\partial t} + rS \frac{\partial F}{\partial S} + \frac{\sigma^2}{2} S^2 \frac{\partial^2 F}{\partial S^2} - rF = 0 \qquad (9.4.6)$$

Note that this equation does not depend on the stock price drift parameter μ, which is the manifestation of the risk-neutral valuation. In other words, investors do not expect a portfolio return exceeding the risk-free interest.

The Black-Scholes equation is the partial differential equation with the first-order derivative in respect to time and the second-order derivative in respect to price. Hence, three boundary conditions determine the Black-Scholes solution. The condition for the time variable is defined with the payoff at maturity. The other two conditions for the price variable are determined with the asymptotic values for the zero and infinite stock prices. For example, price of the put option equals the strike price when the stock price is zero. On the other hand, the put option price tends to be zero if the stock price approaches infinity.

The Black-Scholes equation has an analytic solution in some simple cases. In particular, for the European call option, the Black-Scholes solution is

$$c(S, t) = N(d_1)S(t) - KN(d_2)\exp[-r(T - t)] \qquad (9.4.7)$$

In (9.4.7), $N(x)$ is the standard Gaussian cumulative probability distribution

$$\begin{aligned} d_1 &= [\ln(S/K) + (r + \sigma^2/2)(T - t)]/[\sigma(T - t)^{1/2}], \\ d_2 &= d_1 - (T - t)^{1/2} \end{aligned} \qquad (9.4.8)$$

The Black-Scholes solution for the European put option is

$$p(S, t) = K\exp[-r(T - t)]\, N(-d_2) - S(t)N(-d_1) \qquad (9.4.9)$$

The value of the American call option equals the value of the European call option. However, no analytical expression has been found for the American put option. Numerical methods are widely used for solving the Black-Scholes equation when analytic solution is not available [1–3].

Implied volatility is an important notion related to BST. Usually, the stock volatility used in the Block-Scholes expressions for the option prices, such as (9.4.7), is calculated with the historical stock price data. However, formulation of the inverse problem is also possible. Namely, the market data for the option prices can be used in the left-hand side of (9.4.7) to recover the parameter σ. This parameter is named the implied volatility. Note that there is no analytic expression for implied volatility. Therefore, numerical methods must be employed for its calculation. Several other functions related to the option price, such as *Delta, Gamma,* and *Theta* (so-called *Greeks*), are widely used in the risk management:

$$\Delta = \frac{\partial F}{\partial S}, \ \Gamma = \frac{\partial^2 F}{\partial S^2}, \ \Theta = \frac{\partial F}{\partial t} \qquad (9.4.10)$$

The Black-Scholes equation (9.4.6) can be rewritten in terms of Greeks

$$\Theta + rS\Delta + \frac{\sigma^2}{2} S^2 \Gamma - rF = 0 \qquad (9.4.11)$$

Similarly, Greeks can be defined for the entire portfolio. For example, the portfolio's Delta is $\frac{\partial P}{\partial S}$. Since the share's Delta $\left(\frac{\partial S}{\partial S}\right)$ equals unity, Delta of the portfolio (9.4.3) is zero. Portfolios with zero Delta are called *delta-neutral*. Since Delta depends on both price and time, maintenance of delta-neutral portfolios requires periodic rebalancing, which is also known as *dynamic hedging*. For the European call and put options, Delta equals, respectively

$$\Delta_c = N(d_1), \ \Delta_p = N(d_1) - 1 \qquad (9.4.12)$$

Gamma characterizes the Delta's sensitivity to price variation. If Gamma is small, rebalancing can be performed less frequently. Adding options to the portfolio can change its Gamma. In particular, delta-neutral portfolio with Gamma Γ can be made *gamma-neutral* if it is supplemented with $n = -\Gamma/\Gamma_F$ options having Gamma Γ_F.

Theta characterizes the time decay of the portfolio price. In addition, two other Greeks, *Vega* and *Rho*, are used to measure the portfolio sensitivity to its volatility and risk-free rate, respectively

$$\upsilon = \frac{\partial P}{\partial \sigma}, \ \rho = \frac{\partial P}{\partial r} \qquad (9.4.13)$$

Several assumptions that are made in BST can be easily relaxed. In particular, dividends can be accounted. Also, r and σ can be treated as time-dependent parameters. BST has been expanded in several ways (see [1–3, 7, 8] and references therein). One of the main directions addresses so-called *volatility smile*. The problem is that if all characteristics of the European option besides the strike price are fixed, its implied volatility derived from the Black-Scholes expression is constant. However, real market price volatilities do depend on the strike price, which manifests in "smile-like" graphs. Several approaches have been developed to address this problem. One of them is introducing the time dependencies into the interest rates or/and volatilities (so-called *term structure*). In a different approach, the lognormal stock price distribution is substituted with another statistical distribution. Also, the jump-diffusion stochastic processes are sometimes used instead of the geometric Brownian motion.

Other directions for expanding BST address the market imperfections, such as transaction costs and finite liquidity. Finally, the option price in the current option pricing theory depends on time and price of the underlying asset. This seemingly trivial assumption was questioned in [9]. Namely, it was shown that the option price might depend also on the number of shares of the underlying asset in the arbitrage-free portfolio. Discussion of this paradox is given in the Appendix section of this chapter.

9.5 REFERENCES FOR FURTHER READING

Hull's book is the classical reference for the first reading on financial derivatives [1]. A good introduction to mathematics behind the option theory can be found in [4]. Detailed presentation of the option theory, including exotic options and extensions to BST, is given in [2, 3].

9.6 APPENDIX: THE INVARIANT OF THE ARBITRAGE-FREE PORTFOLIO

As we discussed in Section 9.4, the option price $F(S, t)$ in BST is a function of the stock price and time. The arbitrage-free portfolio in BST consists of one share and of a number of options (M_0) that hedge this share [5]. BST can also be derived with the arbitrage-free portfolio consisting of one option and of a number of shares M_0^{-1} (see, e.g., [1]). However, if the portfolio with an arbitrary number of shares N is considered, and N is treated as an independent variable, that is,

$$F = F(S, t, N) \qquad (9.6.1)$$

then a non-zero derivative, $\partial F / \partial N$, can be recovered within the arbitrage-free paradigm [9]. Since options are traded independently from their underlying assets, the relation (9.6.1) may look senseless to the practitioner. How could this dependence ever come to mind?

Recall the notion of liquidity discussed in Section 2.1. If a market order exceeds supply of an asset at current "best" price, then the order is executed within a price range rather than at a single price. In this case within continuous presentation,

$$S = S(t, N) \qquad (9.6.2)$$

and the expense of buying N shares at time t equals

$$\int_0^N S(t, x)dx \qquad (9.6.3)$$

The liquidity effect in pricing derivatives has been addressed in [10, 11] without proposing (9.6.1). Yet, simply for mathematical generality, one could assume that (9.6.1) may hold if (9.6.2) is valid. Surprisingly, the dependence (9.6.1) holds even for infinite liquidity. Indeed, consider the arbitrage-free portfolio P with an arbitrary number of shares N at price S and M options at price F:

$$P(S, t, N) = NS(t) + MF(S, t, N) \qquad (9.6.4)$$

Let us assume that N is an independent variable and M is a parameter to be defined from the arbitrage-free condition, similar to M_0 in BST. As in BST, the asset price $S = S(t)$ is described with the geometric Brownian process

$$dS = \mu Sdt + \sigma SdW. \qquad (9.6.5)$$

In (9.6.5), μ and σ are the price drift and volatility, and W is the standard Wiener process. According to the Ito's Lemma,

$$dF = \frac{\partial F}{\partial t}dt + \frac{\partial F}{\partial S}dS + \frac{\sigma^2}{2}S^2\frac{\partial^2 F}{\partial S^2}dt + \frac{\partial F}{\partial N}dN \qquad (9.6.6)$$

It follows from (9.6.4) that the portfolio dynamic is

$$dP = MdF + NdS + SdN \qquad (9.6.7)$$

Substituting equation (9.6.6) into equation (9.6.7) yields

$$dP = [M\frac{\partial F}{\partial S} + N]dS + [M\frac{\partial F}{\partial N} + S]dN + M\left[\frac{\partial F}{\partial t} + \frac{\sigma^2}{2}S^2\frac{\partial^2 F}{\partial S^2}\right]dt$$
$$(9.6.8)$$

As within BST, the arbitrage-free portfolio grows with the risk-free interest rate, r

$$dP = rPdt \qquad (9.6.9)$$

Then the combination of equation (9.6.8) and equation (9.6.9) yields

$$[M\frac{\partial F}{\partial S} + N]dS + [M\frac{\partial F}{\partial t} + \frac{\sigma^2}{2}MS^2\frac{\partial^2 F}{\partial S^2} - rMF - rNS]dt +$$
$$[M\frac{\partial F}{\partial N} + S]dN = 0 \qquad (9.6.10)$$

Since equation (9.6.10) must be valid for arbitrary values of dS, dt and dN, it can be split into three equations

$$M\frac{\partial F}{\partial S} + N = 0 \qquad (9.6.11)$$

$$M\left[\frac{\partial F}{\partial t} + \frac{\sigma^2}{2}S^2\frac{\partial^2 F}{\partial S^2} - rF\right] - rNS = 0 \qquad (9.6.12)$$

$$M\frac{\partial F}{\partial N} + S = 0 \qquad (9.6.13)$$

Let us present F(S, t, N) in the form

$$F(S, t, N) = F_0(S, t)Z(N) \qquad (9.6.14)$$

where Z(N) satisfies the condition

$$Z(1) = 1 \qquad (9.6.15)$$

Then it follows from equation (9.6.11) that

$$M = -N/\left(Z\frac{\partial F_0}{\partial S}\right). \qquad (9.6.16)$$

This transforms equation (9.6.15) and equation (9.6.16), respectively, to

$$\frac{\partial F_0}{\partial t} + rS\frac{\partial F_0}{\partial S} + \frac{\sigma^2}{2}S^2\frac{\partial^2 F_0}{\partial S^2} - rF_0 = 0 \qquad (9.6.17)$$

$$\frac{dZ}{dN} = (S/F_0)\frac{\partial F_0}{\partial S}(Z/N), \qquad (9.6.18)$$

Equation (9.6.17) is the classical Black-Scholes equation (cf. with (9.4.6)) while equations (9.6.16) and (9.6.18) define the values of M and Z(N). Solution to equation (9.6.18) that satisfies the condition (9.6.15) is

$$Z(N) = N^a \qquad (9.6.19)$$

where $a = (S/F_0)\Delta$, $\Delta = \dfrac{\partial F_0}{\partial S} = -M_0^{-1}$. Equation (9.6.13) and equation (9.6.16) yield

$$M = -N^{1-a}/\Delta = N^{1-a}M_0 \qquad (9.6.20)$$

Hence, the option price in the arbitrage-free portfolio with N shares equals

$$F(S, t, N) = F_0(S, t)N^a \qquad (9.6.21)$$

It coincides with the BST solution $F_0(S, t)$ only if $N = 1$, that is when the portfolio has one share. However, the total expense of hedging N shares in the arbitrage-free portfolio

$$Q = MF = -(N/\Delta)F_0 = NM_0F_0 \qquad (9.6.22)$$

is the same as within BST. Therefore, Q is the true invariant of the arbitrage-free portfolio.

Invariance of the hedging expense is easy to understand using the dimensionality analysis. Indeed, the arbitrage-free condition (9.6.9) is given in units of the portfolio and therefore can only be used for defining part of the portfolio. Namely, the arbitrage-free condition can be used for defining the hedging expense $Q = MF$ but not for defining both factors M and F. Similarly, the law of energy conservation can be used for defining the kinetic energy of a body, $K = 0.5mV^2$. Yet, this law alone cannot be used for calculating the body's mass, m, and velocity, V. Note, however, that if a body has unit mass ($m = 1$), then the energy conservation law effectively yields the body's velocity. Similarly, the arbitrage-free portfolio with one share does not reveal dependence of the option price on the number of shares in the portfolio.

9.7 EXERCISES

1. (a) Calculate the Black-Scholes prices of the European call and put options with six-month maturity if the current stock price is $20 and grows with average rate of $\mu = 10\%$, volatility is 20%, and risk-free interest rate is 5%. The strike price is: (1) $18; (2) $22.

   (b) How will the results above change if $\mu = 5\%$?

2. Is there an arbitrage opportunity with the following assets: the price of the XYZ stock with no dividends is $100; the European put options at $98 with six-month maturity are sold for $3.50; the European call options at $98 with the same maturity are sold for $8; T-bills with the same maturity are sold for $98. Hint: Check the put-call parity.

**3. Compare the Ito's and Stratonovich's approaches for derivation of the Black-Scholes equation (consult [12]).

Chapter 10

Portfolio Management

This chapter begins with the basic ideas of portfolio selection. Namely, in Section 10.1, the combination of two risky assets and the combination of a risky asset and a risk-free asset are considered. Then two major portfolio management theories are discussed: the capital asset pricing model (Section 10.2) and the arbitrage pricing theory (Section 10.3). Finally, several investment strategies based on exploring market arbitrage opportunities are introduced in Section 10.4.

10.1 PORTFOLIO SELECTION

Optimal investing is an important real-life problem that has been translated into elegant mathematical theories. In general, opportunities for investing include different assets: equities (stocks), bonds, foreign currency, real estate, antique, and others. Here portfolios that contain only financial assets are considered.

There is no single strategy for portfolio selection, because there is always a trade-off between expected return on portfolio and risk of portfolio losses. Risk-free assets such as the U.S. Treasury bills guarantee some return, but it is generally believed that stocks provide higher returns in the long run. The trouble is that the notion of "long run" is doomed to bear an element of uncertainty. Alas, a decade of market growth may end up with a market crash that evaporates a significant part of the equity wealth of an entire generation. Hence, risk aversion (that is often well correlated with investor age) is an important factor in investment strategy.

Portfolio selection has two major steps [1]. First, it is the selection of a combination of risky and risk-free assets and, secondly, it is the selection of risky assets. Let us start with the first step.

For simplicity, consider a combination of one risky asset and one risk-free asset. If the portion of the risky asset in the portfolio is $\alpha(\alpha \leq 1)$, then the expected rate of return equals

$$E[R] = \alpha E[R_r] + (1 - \alpha)R_f = R_f + \alpha(E[R_r] - R_f) \qquad (10.1.1)$$

where R_f and R_r are rates of returns of the risk-free and risky assets, respectively. In the classical portfolio management theory, risk is characterized with the portfolio standard deviation, σ.[1] Since no risk is associated with the risk-free asset, the portfolio risk in our case equals

$$\sigma = \alpha \sigma_r \qquad (10.1.2)$$

Substituting α from (10.1.2) into (10.1.1) yields

$$E[R] = R_f + \sigma(E[R_r] - R_f)/\sigma_r \qquad (10.1.3)$$

The dependence of the expected return on the standard deviation is called the *risk-return trade-off line*. The slope of the straight line (10.1.3)

$$s = (E[R_r] - R_f)/\sigma_r \qquad (10.1.4)$$

is the measure of return in excess of the risk-free return per unit of risk. Obviously, investing in a risky asset makes sense only if $s > 0$, that is, $E[R_r] > R_f$. The risk-return trade-off line defines the *mean-variance efficient portfolio*, that is, the portfolio with the highest expected return at a given risk level.

On the second step of portfolio selection, let us consider the portfolio consisting of two risky assets with returns R_1 and R_2 and with standard deviations σ_1 and σ_2, respectively. If the proportion of the risky asset 1 in the portfolio is $\gamma(\gamma \leq 1)$, then the portfolio rate of return equals

$$E[R] = \gamma E[R_1] + (1 - \gamma)E[R_2] \qquad (10.1.5)$$

and the portfolio standard deviation is

$$\sigma^2 = \gamma^2 \sigma_1{}^2 + (1 - \gamma)^2 \sigma_2{}^2 + 2\gamma(1 - \gamma)\sigma_{12} \qquad (10.1.6)$$

In (10.1.6), σ_{12} is the covariance between the returns of asset 1 and asset 2. For simplicity, it is assumed further that the asset returns are uncorrelated, that is, $\sigma_{12} = 0$. The value of γ that yields minimal risk for this portfolio equals

$$\gamma_m = \sigma_2{}^2/(\sigma_1{}^2 + \sigma_2{}^2), \qquad (10.1.7)$$

This value yields the minimal portfolio risk σ_m

$$\sigma_m{}^2 = \sigma_1{}^2 \sigma_2{}^2/(\sigma_1{}^2 + \sigma_2{}^2) \qquad (10.1.8)$$

Consider an example with $E[R_1] = 0.1$, $E[R_2] = 0.2$, $\sigma_1 = 0.15$, $\sigma_2 = 0.3$. If $\gamma = 0.8$, then $\sigma \approx 0.134 < \sigma_1$ and $E[R] = 0.12 > E[R_1]$. Hence, adding the more risky asset 2 to asset 1 decreases the portfolio risk and increases the portfolio return. This somewhat surprising outcome demonstrates the advantage of portfolio diversification.

Finally, let us combine the risk-free asset with a portfolio that contains two risky assets. The optimal combination of the risky asset portfolio and the risk-free asset can be found at the tangency point between the straight risk-return trade-off line with the intercept $E[R] = R_f$ and the risk-return trade-off curve for the risky asset portfolio (see Figure 10.1). For the portfolio with two risky uncorrelated assets, the proportion γ at the tangency point T equals

$$\gamma_T = (E[R_1] - R_f)\sigma_2{}^2/\{(E[R_1] - R_f)\sigma_2{}^2 + (E[R_2] - R_f)\sigma_1{}^2\} \qquad (10.1.9)$$

Substituting γ_T from (10.1.9) into (10.1.5) and (10.1.6) yields the coordinates of the tangency point (i.e., $E[R_T]$ and σ_T). A similar approach can be used in the general case with an arbitrary number of risky assets. The return $E[R_T]$ for a given portfolio with risk σ_T is "as good as it gets." Is it possible to have returns higher than $E[R_T]$ while investing in the same portfolio? In other words, is it possible to reach say point P on the risk-return trade-off line depicted in Figure. 10.1? Yes, if you *borrow* money at rate R_f and invest it in the portfolio with $\gamma = \gamma_T$. Obviously, the investment risk is then higher than that of σ_T.

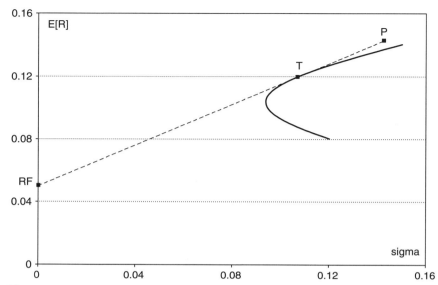

Figure 10.1 The return-risk trade-off lines: portfolio with the risk-free asset and a risky asset (dashed line); portfolio with two risky assets (solid line); $R_f = 0.05$, $\sigma_1 = 0.12$, $\sigma_2 = 0.15$, $E[R_1] = 0.08$, $E[R_2] = 0.14$.

10.2 CAPITAL ASSET PRICING MODEL (CAPM)

The Capital Asset Pricing Model (CAPM) is based on the portfolio selection approach outlined in the previous section. Let us consider the entire universe of risky assets with all possible returns and risks. The set of optimal portfolios in this universe (i.e., portfolios with maximal returns for given risks) forms what is called a *efficient frontier*. The straight line that is tangent to the efficient frontier and has intercept R_f is called the *capital market line*.[2] The tangency point between the capital market line and the efficient frontier corresponds to the so-called *super-efficient portfolio*.

In CAPM, it is assumed that all investors have homogenous expectations of returns, risks, and correlations among the risky assets. It is also assumed that investors behave rationally, meaning they all hold optimal mean-variance efficient portfolios. This implies that all investors have risky assets in their portfolio in the same proportions as the entire market. Hence, CAPM promotes passive investing in the index mutual funds. Within CAPM, the optimal investing strategy is simply choosing a portfolio on the capital market line with acceptable risk level. Therefore, the difference among rational investors is determined only by their risk aversion, which is characterized with the proportion of their wealth allocated to the risk-free assets. Within the CAPM assumptions, it can be shown that the super-efficient portfolio consists of all risky assets weighed with their market values. Such a portfolio is called a *market portfolio.*[3]

CAPM defines the return of a risky asset i with the *security market line*

$$E[R_i] = R_f + \beta_i(E[R_M] - R_f) \qquad (10.2.1)$$

where R_M is the market portfolio return and parameter *beta* β_i equals

$$\beta_i = Cov[R_i, R_M]/Var[R_M] \qquad (10.2.2)$$

Beta defines sensitivity of the risky asset *i* to the market dynamics. Namely, $\beta_i > 1$ means that the asset is more volatile than the entire market while $\beta_i < 1$ implies that the asset has a lower sensitivity to the market movements. The excess return of asset *i* per unit of risk (so-called *Sharpe ratio*) is another criterion widely used for estimation of investment performance

$$S_i = (E[R_i] - R_f)/\sigma_i \qquad (10.2.3)$$

CAPM, being the equilibrium model, has no time dependence. However, econometric analysis based on this model can be conducted providing that the statistical nature of returns is known [2]. It is often assumed that returns are independently and identically distributed. Then the OLS method can be used for estimating β_i in the regression equation for the excess return $Z_i = R_i - R_f$

$$Z_i(t) = \alpha_i + \beta_i Z_M(t) + \varepsilon_i(t) \qquad (10.2.4)$$

It is usually assumed that $\varepsilon_i(t)$ is a normal process and the S&P 500 Index is the benchmark for the market portfolio return $R_M(t)$. More details on the CAPM validation and the general results for the mean-variance efficient portfolios can be found in [2, 3].

As indicated above, CAPM is based on the belief that investing in risky assets yields average returns higher than the risk-free return. Hence, the rationale for investing in risky assets becomes questionable in bear markets. Another problem is that the asset diversification advocated by CAPM is helpful if returns of different assets are uncorrelated. Unfortunately, correlations between asset returns may grow in bear markets [4]. Besides the failure to describe prolonged bear markets, another disadvantage of CAPM is its high sensitivity to proxy for the market portfolio. The latter drawback implies that CAPM is accurate only conditionally, within a given time period, where the state variables that determine economy are fixed [2]. Then it seems natural to extend CAPM to a multifactor model.

10.3 ARBITRAGE PRICING THEORY (APT)

The CAPM equation (10.2.1) implies that return on risky assets is determined only by a single non-diversifiable risk, namely by the risk associated with the entire market. The Arbitrage Pricing Theory (APT) offers a generic extension of CAPM into the multifactor paradigm.

APT is based on two postulates. First, the return for an asset i ($i = 1, \ldots, N$) at every time period is a weighed sum of the risk factor contributions $f_j(t)$ ($j = 1, \ldots, K$, $K < N$) plus an asset-specific component $\varepsilon_i(t)$

$$R_i(t) = a_i + \beta_{i1}f_1 + \beta_{i2}f_2 + \ldots + \beta_{iK}f_K + \varepsilon_i(t) \qquad (10.3.1)$$

In (10.3.1), β_{ij} are the factor weights (betas). It is assumed that the expectations of all factor values and for the asset-specific innovations are zero

$$E[f_1(t)] = E[f_2(t)] = \ldots = E[f_K(t)] = E[\varepsilon_i(t)] = 0 \qquad (10.3.2)$$

Also, the time distributions of the risk factors and asset-specific innovations are independent

$$Cov[f_j(t), f_j(t')] = 0, \ Cov[\varepsilon_i(t), \varepsilon_i(t')] = 0, \ t \neq t' \qquad (10.3.3)$$

and uncorrelated

$$Cov[f_j(t), \varepsilon_i(t)] = 0 \qquad (10.3.4)$$

Within APT, the correlations between the risk factors and the asset-specific innovations may exist, that is $Cov[f_j(t), f_k(t)]$ and $Cov[\varepsilon_i(t), \varepsilon_j(t)]$ may differ from zero.

The second postulate of APT requires that there are no arbitrage opportunities. This implies, in particular, that any portfolio in which all factor contributions are canceled out must have return equal to that of the risk-free asset (see Exercise 3). These two postulates lead to the APT theorem (see, e.g., [5]). In its simple form, it states that there exist such $K + 1$ constants $\lambda_0, \lambda_1, \ldots \lambda_K$ (not all of them equal zero) that

$$E[R_i(t)] = \lambda_0 + \beta_{i1}\lambda_1 + \ldots + \beta_{iK}\lambda_K \qquad (10.3.5)$$

While λ_0 has the sense of the risk-free asset return, the numbers λ_j are named the risk premiums for the j-th risk factors.

Let us define a *well-diversified portfolio* as a portfolio that consists of N assets with the weights w_i where $\sum_{i=1}^{N} w_i = 1$, so that $w_i < W/N$ and $W \approx 1$ is a constant. Hence, the specific of a well-diversified portfolio is that it is not overweighed by any of its asset components.

APT turns out to be more accurate for well-diversified portfolios than for individual stocks. The general APT states that if the return of a well-diversified portfolio equals

$$R(t) = a + \beta_1 f_1 + \beta_2 f_2 + \ldots + \beta_K f_K + \varepsilon(t) \qquad (10.3.6)$$

where

$$a = \sum_{i=1}^{N} w_i a_i, \quad \beta_i = \sum_{k=1}^{N} w_k \beta_{ik} \qquad (10.3.7)$$

then the expected portfolio return is

$$E[R(t)] = \lambda_0 + \beta_1 \lambda_1 + \ldots + \beta_K \lambda_K \qquad (10.3.8)$$

In addition, the returns of the assets that constitute the portfolio satisfy the simple APT (10.3.5).

APT does not specify the risk factors. Yet, the essential sources of risk are well described in the literature [6]. They include both macro-economic factors including inflation risk, interest rate, and corporate factors, for example, Return on Equity (ROE).[4] Development of statistically reliable multifactor portfolio models poses significant challenges [2]. Yet, multifactor models are widely used in active portfolio management.

Both CAPM and APT consider only one time period and treat the risk-free interest rate as an exogenous parameter. However, in real life, investors make investing and consumption decisions that are in effect for long periods of time. An interesting direction in the portfolio theory (that is beyond the scope of this book) describes investment and consumption processes within a single framework. The risk-free interest rate is then determined by the consumption growth and by investor risk aversion. The most prominent theories in this direction are the intertemporal CAPM (ICAPM) and the consumption CAPM (CCAPM) [2, 3, 7].

10.4 ARBITRAGE TRADING STRATEGIES

The simple investment strategy means "buy and hold" securities of "good" companies until their performance worsens, then sell them and buy better assets. A more sophisticated approach is sensitive to changing economic environment and an investor's risk tolerance, which implies periodic rebalancing of the investor portfolio between cash, fixed income, and equities. Proponents of the conservative investment strategy believe that this is everything an investor should do while investing for the "long run." Yet, many investors are not satisfied with the long-term expectations: they want to make money at all times (and who could blame them?). Several concepts being intensively explored by a number of financial institutions, particularly by the hedge funds, are called *market-neutral strategies*. In a nutshell, market-neutral strategy implies hedging the risk of financial losses by combining long and short positions in the portfolio. For example, consider two companies within the same industry, A and B, one of which (A) yields consistently higher returns. The strategy named *pair trading* involves simultaneously buying shares A and short selling shares B. Obviously, if the entire sector rises, this strategy does not bring as much money as simply buying shares A. However, if the entire market falls, presumably shares B will have higher losses than shares A. Then the profits from short selling shares B would more than compensate for the losses from buying shares A.

Specifics of the hedging strategies are not widely advertised for obvious reasons: the more investors target the same market inefficiency, the faster it is wiped out. Several directions in the market-neutral investing are described in the literature [8].

Convertible arbitrage. Convertible bonds are bonds that can be converted into shares of the same company. Convertible bonds often decline less in a falling market than shares of the same company do. Hence, the idea of the convertible arbitrage is buying convertible bonds and short selling the underlying stocks.

Fixed-income arbitrage. This strategy implies taking long and short positions in different fixed-income securities. By watching the correlations between different securities, one can buy those securities that seem to become underpriced and sell short those that look overpriced.

Mortgage-backed securities (MBS) arbitrage. MBS is actually a form of fixed income with a prepayment option. Yet, there are so many different MBS that this makes them a separate business.

Merger arbitrage. This form of arbitrage involves buying shares of a company that is being bought and short selling the shares of the buying company. The rationale behind this strategy is that companies are usually acquired at a premium, which sends down the stock prices of acquiring companies.

Equity hedge. This strategy is not exactly the market-neutral one, as the ratio between long and short equity positions may vary depending on the market conditions. Sometimes one of the positions is the stock index future while the other positions are the stocks that constitute this index (so-called *index arbitrage*). Pair trading also fits this strategy.

Equity market-neutral strategy and statistical arbitrage. Nicholas discerns these two strategies by the level of constraints (availability of resources) imposed upon the portfolio manager [8]. The common feature of these strategies is that (in contrast to the equity hedge), they require complete offsetting of the long positions by the short positions. Statistical arbitrage implies fewer constraints in the development of quantitative models and hence a lower amount of the portfolio manager's discretion in constructing a portfolio.

Relative value arbitrage. This is a synthetic approach that may embrace several hedging strategies and different securities including equities, bonds, options, and foreign currencies. Looking for the arbitrage opportunities "across the board" is technically more challenging but potentially rewarding.

Some academic research on efficiency of the arbitrage trading strategies can be found in [9–12] and references therein. Note that the research methodology in this field is itself a non-trivial problem [13].

10.5 REFERENCES FOR FURTHER READING

A good introduction into the finance theory, including CAPM, is given in [1]. For a description of the portfolio theory and investment science with an increasing level of technical detail, see [5, 14].

10.6 EXERCISES

1. Consider a portfolio with two assets having the following returns and standard deviations: $E[R_1] = 0.15$, $E[R_2] = 0.1$, $\sigma_1 = 0.2$, $\sigma_2 = 0.15$. The proportion of asset 1 in the portfolio $\gamma = 0.5$. Calculate the portfolio return and standard deviation. The correlation coefficient between assets is (a) 0.5; (b) -0.5.

2. Consider returns of stock A and the market portfolio M in three years:

A	-7%	12%	26%
M	-5%	9%	18%

   Assuming the risk-free rate is 5%, (a) calculate β of stock A; and (b) verify if CAPM describes pricing of stock A.

3. Providing the stock returns follow the two-factor APT: $R_i(t) = a_i + \beta_{i1} f_1 + \beta_{i2} f_2 + \varepsilon_i(t)$, construct a portfolio with three stocks (i.e., define w_1, w_2, and $w_3 = 1 - w_1 - w_2$) that yields return equal to that of the risk-free asset.

4. Providing the stock returns follow the two-factor simple APT, derive the values of the risk premiums. Assume the expected returns of two stocks and the risk-free rate are equal to R_1, R_2, and R_f, respectively.

Chapter 11

Market Risk Measurement

The widely used risk measure, value at risk (VaR), is discussed in Section 11.1. Furthermore, the notion of the coherent risk measure is introduced and one such popular measure, namely expected tail losses (ETL), is described. In Section 11.2, various approaches to calculating risk measures are discussed.

11.1 RISK MEASURES

There are several possible causes of financial losses. First, there is *market risk* that results from unexpected changes in the market prices, interest rates, or foreign exchange rates. Other types of risk relevant to financial risk management include *liquidity risk*, *credit risk*, and *operational risk* [1]. The liquidity risk closely related to market risk is determined by a finite number of assets available at a given price (see discussion in Section 2.1). Another form of liquidity risk (so-called *cash-flow risk*) refers to the inability to pay off a debt in time. Credit risk arises when one of the counterparts involved in a financial transaction does not fulfill its obligation. Finally, *operational risk* is a generic notion for unforeseen human and technical problems, such as fraud, accidents, and so on. Here we shall focus exclusively on measurement of the market risk.

In Chapter 10, we discussed risk measures such as the asset return variance and the CAPM beta. Several risk factors used in APT were also mentioned. At present, arguably the most widely used risk measure is *value at risk* (VaR) [1]. In short, VaR refers to the maximum amount of an asset that is likely to be lost over a given period at a specific confidence level. This implies that the probability density function for *profits and losses* $(P/L)^1$ is known. In the simplest case, this distribution is normal

$$P_N(x) = \frac{1}{\sqrt{2\pi}\sigma} \exp\left[-(x - \mu)^2/2\sigma^2\right] \qquad (11.1.1)$$

where μ and σ are the mean and standard deviation, respectively. Then for the chosen confidence level α,

$$VAR(\alpha) = -\sigma z_\alpha - \mu \qquad (11.1.2)$$

The value of z_α can be determined from the cumulative distribution function for the standard normal distribution (3.2.10)

$$\Pr(Z < z_\alpha) = \int_{-\infty}^{z_\alpha} \frac{1}{\sqrt{2\pi}} \exp\left[-z^2/2\right]dz = 1 - \alpha \qquad (11.1.3)$$

Since $z_\alpha < 0$ at $\alpha > 50\%$, the definition (11.1.2) implies that positive values of VaR point to losses. In general, VaR(α) grows with the confidence level α. Sufficiently high values of the mean P/L $(\mu > -\sigma z_\alpha)$ for given α move VaR(α) into the negative region, which implies profits rather than losses. Examples of z_α for typical values of $\alpha = 95\%$ and $\alpha = 99\%$ are given in Figure 11.1. Note that the return variance σ corresponds to $z_\alpha = -1$ and yields $\alpha \approx 84\%$.

The advantages of VaR are well known. VaR is a simple and universal measure that can be used for determining risks of different financial assets and entire portfolios. Still, VaR has some drawbacks [2]. First, accuracy of VaR is determined by the model assumptions and is rather sensitive to implementation. Also, VaR provides an estimate for losses within a given confidence interval α but says nothing about possible outcomes outside this interval. A somewhat paradoxical feature of VaR is that it can discourage investment diversification. Indeed, adding volatile assets to a portfolio may move VaR above the chosen risk threshold. Another problem with VaR is that it can violate the sub-additivity rule for portfolio risk. According to this rule, the risk measure ρ must satisfy the condition

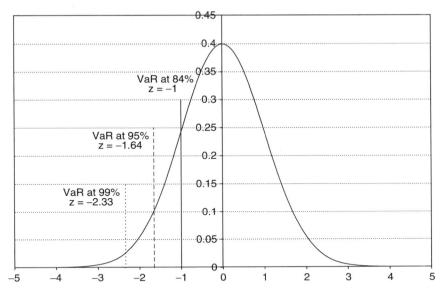

Figure 11.1 VaR for the standard normal probability distribution of P/L.

$$\rho(A + B) \le \rho(A) + \rho(B) \qquad (11.1.4)$$

which means the risk of owning the sum of two assets must not be higher than the sum of the individual risks of these assets. The condition (11.1.4) immediately yields an upper estimate of combined risk. Violation of the sub-additivity rule may lead to several problems. In particular, it may provoke investors to establish separate accounts for every asset they have. Unfortunately, VaR satisfies (11.1.4) only if the probability density function for P/L is normal (or, more generally, elliptical) [3].

The generic criterions for the risk measures that satisfy the requirements of the modern risk management are formulated in [3]. Besides the sub-additivity rule (11.1.4), they include the following conditions.

$$\rho(\lambda A) = \lambda \rho(A), \ \lambda > 0 \ \text{(homogeneity)} \qquad (11.1.5)$$

$$\rho(A) \le \rho(B), \ \text{if} \ A \le B \ \text{(monotonicity)} \qquad (11.1.6)$$

$$\rho(A + C) = \rho(A) - C \ \text{(translation invariance)} \qquad (11.1.7)$$

In (11.1.7), C represents a risk-free amount. Adding this amount to a risky portfolio should decrease the total risk, since this amount is not subjected to potential losses. The risk measures that satisfy the conditions (11.1.4)–(11.1.7) are called *coherent risk measures*. It can be shown that any coherent risk measure represents the maximum of the expected loss on a set of "generalized scenarios" where every such scenario is determined with its value of loss and probability of occurrence [3]. This result yields the coherent risk measure called *expected tail loss* (ETL).[2]

$$ETL = E[L|L > VaR] \qquad (11.1.8)$$

While VaR is an estimate of loss within a given confidence level, ETL is an estimate of loss within the remaining tail. For a given probability distribution of P/L and a given α, ETL is always higher than VaR (cf. Figures 11.1 and 11.2).

ETL has several important advantages over VaR [2]. In short, ETL provides an estimate for an average "worst case scenario" while VaR only gives a possible loss within a chosen confidence interval. ETL has all the benefits of the coherent risk measure and does not discourage risk diversification. Finally, ETL turns out to be a more convenient measure for solving the portfolio optimization problem.

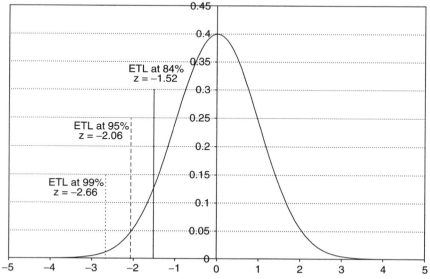

Figure 11.2 ETL for the standard normal probability distribution of P/L.

11.2 CALCULATING RISK

Two main approaches are used for calculating VaR and ETL [2]. First, there is *historical simulation*, a non-parametric approach that employs historical data. Consider a sample of 100 P/L values as a simple example for calculating VaR and ETL. Let us choose the confidence level of 95%. Then VaR is the sixth smallest number in the sample while ETL is the average of the five smallest numbers within the sample. In the general case of N observations, VaR at the confidence level α is the $[N(1 - \alpha) + 1]$ lowest observation and ETL is the average of $N(1 - \alpha)$ smallest observations.

The well-known problem with the historical simulation is handling of old data. First, "too old" data may lose their relevance. Therefore, moving data windows (i.e., fixed number of observations prior to every new period) are often used. Another subject of concern is outliers. Different data weighting schemes are used to address this problem. In a simple approach, the historical data $X(t - k)$ are multiplied by the factor λ^k where $0 < \lambda < 1$. Another interesting idea is weighting the historical data with their volatility [4]. Namely, the asset returns $R(t)$ at time t used in forecasting VaR for time T are scaled with the volatility ratio

$$R'(t) = R(t)\sigma(T)/\sigma(t) \qquad (11.2.1)$$

where $\sigma(t)$ is the historical forecast of the asset volatility.[3] As a result, the actual return at day t is increased if the volatility forecast at day T is higher than that of day t, and vice versa. The scaled forecasts $R'(t)$ are further used in calculating VaR in the same way as the forecasts $R(t)$ are used in equal-weight historical simulation. Other more sophisticated non-parametric techniques are discussed in [2] and references therein.

An obvious advantage of the non-parametric approaches is their relative conceptual and implementation simplicity. The main disadvantage of the non-parametric approaches is their absolute dependence on the historical data: Collecting and filtering empirical data always comes at a price.

The parametric approach is a plausible alternative to historical simulation. This approach is based on fitting the P/L probability distribution to some analytic function. The (log)normal, Student

and extreme value distributions are commonly used in modeling P/L
[2, 5]. The parametric approach is easy to implement since the analytic
expressions can often be used. In particular, the assumption of the
normal distribution reduces calculating VaR to (11.1.2). Also, VaR
for time interval T can be easily expressed via VaR for unit time (e.g.,
via daily VaR (DVaR) providing T is the number of days)

$$VaR(T) = DVaR\sqrt{T} \qquad (11.2.2)$$

VaR for a portfolio of N assets is calculated using the variance of the
multivariate normal distribution

$$\sigma_N{}^2 = \sum_{i, j=1}^{N} \sigma_{ij} \qquad (11.2.3)$$

If the P/L distribution is normal, ETL can also be calculated analyt-
ically

$$ETL(\alpha) = \sigma P_{SN}(Z_\alpha)/(1 - \alpha) - \mu \qquad (11.2.4)$$

The value z_α in (11.2.4) is determined with (11.1.3). Obviously, the
parametric approach is as good and accurate as the choice of the
analytic probability distribution.

Calculating VaR has become a part of the regulatory environment
in the financial industry [6]. As a result, several methodologies have
been developed for testing the accuracy of VaR models. The most
widely used method is the Kupiec test. This test is based on the
assumption that if the VaR(α) model is accurate, the number of the
tail losses n in a sample N is determined with the binomial distribution

$$P_B(n; N, 1 - \alpha) = \frac{N!}{n!(N - n)!}(1 - \alpha)^n \alpha^{(N-n)} \qquad (11.2.5)$$

The null hypothesis is that n/N equals $1 - \alpha$, which can be tested with
the relevant likelihood ratio statistic. The Kupiec test has clear meaning but may be inaccurate for not very large data samples. Other
approaches for testing the VaR models are described in [2, 6] and
references therein.

11.3 REFERENCES FOR FURTHER READING

The Jorion's monograph [1] is a popular reference for VaR-based risk management. The Dowd's textbook [2] is a good resource for the modern risk measurement approaches beyond VaR.

11.4 EXERCISES

1. Consider a portfolio with two assets: asset 1 has current value $1 million and annual volatility 12%; asset 2 has current value $2 million and annual volatility 24%. Assuming that returns are normally distributed and there are 250 working days per year, calculate 5-day VaR of this portfolio with 99% confidence level. Perform calculations for the asset correlation coefficient equal to (a) 0.5 and (b) −0.5.
2. Verify (11.2.4).
*3. Implement the algorithm of calculating ETL for given P/L density function. Analyze the algorithm accuracy as a function of the number of integration points by comparing the calculation results with the analytic expression for the normal distribution (11.2.4).

Chapter 12

Agent-Based Modeling of Financial Markets

12.1 INTRODUCTION

Agent-based modeling has become a popular methodology in social sciences, particularly in economics.[1] Here we focus on the agent-based modeling of financial markets [1]. The very idea of describing markets with models of interacting agents (traders, investors) does not fit well with the classical financial theory that is based on the notions of efficient markets and rational investors. However, it has become obvious that investors are neither perfectly rational nor have homogeneous expectations of the market trends (see also Section 2.3). Agent-based modeling proves to be a flexible framework for a realistic description of the investor adaptation and decision-making process.

The paradigm of agent-based modeling applied to financial markets implies that trader actions determine price. This concept is similar to that of statistical physics within which the thermodynamic (macroscopic) properties of the medium are described via molecular interactions. A noted expansion of the microscopic modeling methodology into social systems is the *minority game* (see [2] and references therein). Its development was inspired by the famous El Farol's bar problem [3]. This problem considers a number of patrons N willing to attend a bar with a number of seats N_s. It is assumed that $N_s < N$ and every patron prefers to stay at home if he expects that the number of people attending the bar will exceed N_s. There is no communication among patrons and they make decisions using only information on past attendance and different predictors (e.g., attendance today is the same as yesterday, or is some average of past attendance).

The minority game is a simple binary choice problem in which players have to choose between two sides, and those on the minority side win. Similarly to the El Farol's bar problem, in the minority game there is no communication among players and only a given set of forecasting strategies defines player decisions. The minority game is an interesting stylized model that may have some financial implications [2]. But we shall focus further on the models derived specifically for describing financial markets.

In the known literature, early work on the agent-based modeling of financial markets can be traced back to 1980 [4]. In this paper, Beja and Goldman considered two major trading strategies, value investing and trend following. In particular, they showed that system equilibrium may become unstable when the number of trend followers grows.

Since then, many agent-based models of financial markets have been developed (see, e.g., reviews [1, 5], the recent collection [6] and references therein). We divide these models into two major groups. In the first group, agents make decisions based on their own predictions of future prices and adapt their beliefs using different predictor functions of past returns. The principal feature of this group is that price is derived from the supply-demand equilibrium [7–10].[2] Therefore, we call this group the *adaptive equilibrium models*. In the other group, the assumption of the equilibrium price is not employed. Instead, price is assumed to be a dynamic variable determined via its empirical relation to the excess demand (see, e.g., [11, 12]). We call this group the *non-equilibrium price models*. In the following two sections, we discuss two instructive examples for both groups of models, respectively. Finally, Section 12.4 describes a non-equilibrium price model that is derived exclusively in terms of observable variables [13].

12.2 ADAPTIVE EQUILIBRIUM MODELS

In this group of models [7–10], agents can invest either in the risk-free asset (bond) or in the risky asset (e.g., a stock market index). The risk-free asset is assumed to have an infinite supply and a constant interest rate. Agents attempt to maximize their wealth by using some risk aversion criterion. Predictions of future return are adapted using past returns. The solution to the wealth maximization problem yields the investor demand for the risky asset. This demand in turn determines the asset price in equilibrium. Let us formalize these assumptions using the notations from [10]. The return on the risky asset at time t is defined as

$$\rho_t = (p_t - p_{t-1} + y_t)/p_{t-1} \qquad (12.2.1)$$

where p_t and y_t are (ex-dividend) price and dividend of one share of the risky asset, respectively. Wealth dynamics of agent i is given by

$$W_{i,t+1} = R(1 - \pi_{i,t})W_{i,t} + \pi_{i,t}W_{i,t}(1 + \rho_{t+1})$$
$$= W_{i,t}[R + \pi_{i,t}(\rho_{t+1} - r)] \qquad (12.2.2)$$

where r is the interest rate of the risk-free asset, $R = 1 + r$, and $\pi_{i,t}$ is the proportion of wealth of agent i invested in the risky asset at time t. Every agent is assumed to be a taker of the risky asset at price that is established in the demand-supply equilibrium. Let us denote $E_{i,t}$ and $V_{i,t}$ the "beliefs" of trader i at time t about the conditional expectation of wealth and the conditional variance of wealth, respectively. It follows from (12.2.2) that

$$E_{i,t}[W_{i,t+1}] = W_{i,t}[R + \pi_{i,t}(E_{i,t}[\rho_{t+1}] - r)], \qquad (12.2.3)$$
$$V_{i,t}[W_{i,t+1}] = \pi_{i,t}^2 W_{i,t}^2 V_{i,t}[\rho_{t+1}] \qquad (12.2.4)$$

Also, every agent i believes that return of the risky asset is normally distributed with mean $E_{i,t}[\rho_{t+1}]$ and variance $V_{i,t}[\rho_{t+1}]$. Agents choose the proportion $\pi_{i,t}$ of their wealth to invest in the risky asset, which maximizes the utility function U

$$\max_{\pi_{i,t}} \{E_{i,t}[U(W_{i,t+1})]\} \qquad (12.2.5)$$

The utility function chosen in [9, 10] is

$$U(W_{i,t}) = \log(W_{i,t}) \qquad (12.2.6)$$

Then demand $\pi_{i,t}$ that satisfies (12.2.5) equals

$$\pi_{i,t} = \frac{E_{i,t}[\rho_{t+1}] - r}{V_{i,t}[\rho_{t+1}]} \qquad (12.2.7)$$

Another utility function used in the adaptive equilibrium models employs the so-called *constant absolute risk aversion (CARA) function* [7, 8]

$$U(W_{i,t}) = E_{i,t}[W_{i,t+1}] - \frac{a}{2}V_{i,t}[W_{i,t+1}] \qquad (12.2.8)$$

where a is the risk aversion constant. For the constant conditional variance $V_{i,t} = \sigma^2$, the CARA function yields the demand

$$\pi_{i,t} = \frac{E_{i,t}[\rho_{t+1}] - r}{a\sigma^2} \qquad (12.2.9)$$

The number of shares of the risky asset that corresponds to demand $\pi_{i,t}$ equals

$$N_{i,t} = \pi_{i,t}W_{i,t}/p_t \qquad (12.2.10)$$

Since the total number of shares assumed to be fixed $\left(\sum_i N_{i,t} = N = \text{const}\right)$, the market-clearing price equals

$$p_t = \frac{1}{N}\sum_i \pi_{i,t}\, W_{i,t} \qquad (12.2.11)$$

The adaptive equilibrium model described so far does not contradict the classical asset pricing theory. The new concept in this model is the heterogeneous beliefs. In its general form [7, 10]

$$E_{i,t}[\rho_{t+1}] = f_i(\rho_{t-1}, \dots, \rho_{t-Li}), \qquad (12.2.12)$$

$$V_{i,t}[\rho_{t+1}] = g_i(\rho_{t-1}, \dots, \rho_{t-Li}) \qquad (12.2.13)$$

The deterministic functions f_i and g_i depend on past returns with lags up to L_i and may vary for different agents.[3]

   While variance is usually assumed to be constant ($g_i = \sigma^2$), several trading strategies f_i are discussed in the literature. First, there are fundamentalists who use analysis of the business fundamentals to make their forecasts on the risk premium δ_F

$$E_{F,t}[\rho_{t+1}] = r + \delta_F \qquad (12.2.14)$$

In simple models, the risk premium $\delta_F > 0$ is a constant but it can be a function of time and/or variance in the general case. Another major strategy is momentum trading (traders who use it are often called *chartists*). Momentum traders use history of past returns to make their forecasts. Namely, their strategy can be described as

$$E_{M,\,t}[\rho_{t+1}] = r + \delta_M + \sum_{k=1}^{L} a_k \rho_{t-k} \qquad (12.2.15)$$

where $\delta_M > 0$ is the constant component of the momentum risk premium and $a_k > 0$ are the weights of past returns ρ_{t-k}. Finally, *contrarians* employ the strategy that is formally similar to the momentum strategy

$$E_{C,\,t}[\rho_{t+1}] = r + \delta_C + \sum_{k=1}^{L} b_k \rho_{t-k} \qquad (12.2.16)$$

with the principal difference that all b_k are negative. This implies that contrarians expect the market to turn around (e.g., from bull market to bear market).

An important feature of adaptive equilibrium models is that agents are able to analyze performance of different strategies and choose the most efficient one. Since these strategies have limited accuracy, such adaptability is called *bounded rationality*.

In the limit of infinite number of agents, Brock and Hommes offer a discrete analog of the Gibbs probability distribution for the fraction of traders with the strategy i [7]

$$n_{it} = \exp\left[\beta(\Phi_{i,\,t-1} - C_i)\right]/Z_t, \ Z_t = \sum_i \exp\left[\beta(\Phi_{i,\,t-1} - C_i)\right] \quad (12.2.17)$$

In (12.2.17), $C_i \geq 0$ is the cost of the strategy i, the parameter β is called the intensity of choice, and $\Phi_{i,\,t}$ is the fitness function that characterizes the efficiency of strategy i. The natural choice for the fitness function is

$$\Phi_{i,\,t} = \gamma\Phi_{i,\,t-1} + \varphi_{i,\,t}, \ \varphi_{i,\,t} = \pi_{i,\,t}(W_{i,\,t} - W_{i,\,t-1})/W_{i,\,t-1} \quad (12.2.18)$$

where $0 \leq \gamma \leq 1$ is the memory parameter that retains part of past performance in the current strategy.

Adaptive equilibrium models have been studied in several directions. Some work has focused on analytic analysis of simpler models. In particular, the system stability and routes to chaos have been discussed in [7, 10]. In the meantime, extensive computational modeling has been performed in [9] and particularly for the so-called *Santa Fe artificial market*, in which a significant number of trading strategies were implemented [8].

12.3 NON-EQUILIBRIUM PRICE MODELS

The concept of market clearing that is used in determining price of the risky asset in the adaptive equilibrium models does not accurately reflect the way real markets work. In fact, the number of shares involved in trading varies with time, and price is essentially a dynamic variable. A simple yet reasonable alternative to the price-clearing paradigm is the equation of price formation that is based on the empirical relation between price change and excess demand [4].

Different agent decision-making rules may be implemented within this approach. Here the elaborated model offered by Lux [11] is described. In this model, two groups of agents, namely chartists and fundamentalists, are considered. Agents can compare the efficiency of different trading strategies and switch from one strategy to another. Therefore, the numbers of chartists, $n_c(t)$, and fundamentalists, $n_f(t)$, vary with time while the total number of agents in the market N is assumed constant. The chartist group in turn is sub-divided into optimistic (bullish) and pessimistic (bearish) traders with the numbers $n_+(t)$ and $n_-(t)$, respectively

$$n_c(t) + n_f(t) = N, \quad n_+(t) + n_-(t) = n_c(t) \qquad (12.3.1)$$

Several aspects of trader behavior are considered. First, the chartist decisions are affected by the peer opinion (so-called *mimetic contagion*). Secondly, traders change strategy while seeking optimal performance. Finally, traders may exit and enter markets. The bullish chartist dynamics is formalized in the following way:

$$
\begin{aligned}
dn_+/dt = {} & (n_-p_{+-} - n_+p_{-+})(1 - n_f/N) + && \text{mimetic contagion} \\
& n_f n_+ (p_{+f} - p_{f+})/N + && \text{changes of strategy} \\
& (b - a)n_+ && \text{market entry and exit} \qquad (12.3.2)
\end{aligned}
$$

Here, $p_{\alpha\beta}$ denotes the probability of transition from group β to group α. Similarly, the bearish chartist dynamics is given by

$$
\begin{aligned}
dn_-/dt = {} & (n_+p_{-+} - n_-p_{+-})(1 - n_f/N) + && \text{mimetic contagion} \\
& n_f n_- (p_{-f} - p_{f-})/N + && \text{changes of strategy} \\
& (b - a)n_- && \text{market entry and exit} \qquad (12.3.3)
\end{aligned}
$$

It is assumed that traders entering the market start with the chartist strategy. Therefore, constant total number of traders yields the relation $b = aN/n_c$. Equations (12.3.1)–(12.3.3) describe the dynamics of three trader groups (n_f, n_+, n_-) assuming that all transfer probabilities $p_{\alpha\beta}$ are determined. The change between the chartist bullish and bearish mood is given by

$$p_{+-} = 1/p_{-+} = v_1 \exp(-U_1),$$
$$U_1 = \alpha_1(n_+ - n_-)/n_c + (\alpha_2/v_1)dP/dt \qquad (12.3.4)$$

where v_1, α_1 and α_2 are parameters and P is price. Conversion of fundamentalists into bullish chartists and back is described with

$$p_{+f} = 1/p_{f+} = v_2 \exp(-U_{21}),$$
$$U_{21} = \alpha_3((r + v_2^{-1}dP/dt)/P - R - s|(P_f - P)/P|) \qquad (12.3.5)$$

where v_2 and α_3 are parameters, r is the stock dividend, R is the average revenue of economy, s is a discounting factor $0 < s < 1$, and P_f is the fundamental price of the risky asset assumed to be an input parameter. Similarly, conversion of fundamentalists into bearish chartists and back is given by

$$p_{-f} = 1/p_{f-} = v_2 \exp(-U_{22}),$$
$$U_{22} = \alpha_3(R - (r + v_2^{-1}dP/dt)/P - s|(P_f - P)/P|) \qquad (12.3.6)$$

Price P in (12.3.4)–(12.3.6) is a variable that still must be defined. Hence, an additional equation is needed in order to close the system (12.3.1)–(12.3.6). As it was noted previously, an empirical relation between the price change and the excess demand constitutes the specific of the non-equilibrium price models[4]

$$dP/dt = \beta D_{ex} \qquad (12.3.7)$$

In the model [11], the excess demand equals

$$D_{ex} = t_c(n_+ - n_-) + \gamma n_f(P_f - P) \qquad (12.3.8)$$

The first and second terms in the right-hand side of (12.3.8) are the excess demands of the chartists and fundamentalists, respectively; β, t_c and γ are parameters.

The system (12.3.1)–(12.3.8) has rich dynamic properties determined by its input parameters. The system solutions include stable equilibrium, periodic patterns, and chaotic attractors. Interestingly, the distributions of returns derived from the chaotic trajectories may have fat tails typical for empirical data. Particularly in [14], the model [11] was modified to describe the arrival of news in the market, which affects the fundamental price. This process was modeled with the Gaussian random variable $\varepsilon(t)$ so that

$$\ln P_f(t) - \ln P_f(t-1) = \varepsilon(t) \qquad (12.3.9)$$

The modeling results exhibited the power-law scaling and temporal volatility dependence in the price distributions.

12.4 THE OBSERVABLE VARIABLES MODEL

12.4.1 THE FRAMEWORK

The models discussed so far are capable of reproducing important features of financial market dynamics. Yet, one may notice a degree of arbitrariness in this field. The number of different agent types and the rules of their transition and adaptation vary from one model to another. Also, little is known about optimal choice of the model parameters [15, 16]. As a result, many interesting properties, such as deterministic chaos, may be the model artifacts rather than reflections of the real world.[5]

A parsimonious approach to choosing variables in the agent-based modeling of financial markets was offered in [17]. Namely, it was suggested to derive agent-based models exclusively in terms of observable variables. Note that the notion of observable data in finance should be discerned from the notion of publicly available data. While the transaction prices in regulated markets are publicly available, the market microstructure is not (see Section 2.1). Still, every event in the financial markets that affects the market microstructure (such as quote submission, quote cancellation, transactions, etc.) is recorded and stored for business and legal purposes. This information allows one to reconstruct the market microstructure at every moment. We define observable variables in finance as those that can be retrieved or calculated from the records of market events. Whether these records are publicly available at present is a secondary issue. More importantly, these data exist and can therefore potentially be used for calibrating and testing the theoretical models.

The numbers of agents of different types generally are not observable. Indeed, consider a market analog of "Maxwell's Demon" who is able to instantly parse all market events. The Demon cannot discern "chartists" and "fundamentalists" in typical situations, such as when the current price, being lower than the fundamental price, is growing. In this case, all traders buy rather than sell. Similarly, when the current price, being higher than the fundamental price, is falling, all traders sell rather than buy.

Only price, the total number of buyers, and the total number of sellers are always observable. Whether a trader becomes a buyer or seller can be defined by mixing different behavior patterns in the trader decision-making rule. Let us describe a simple non-equilibrium price model derived along these lines [17]. We discern "buyers" $(+)$ and "sellers" $(-)$. Total number of traders is N

$$N_+(t) + N_-(t) = N \qquad (12.4.1)$$

The scaled numbers of buyers, $n_+(t) = N_+(t)/N$, and sellers, $n_-(t) = N_-(t)/N$, are described with equations

$$dn_+/dt = v_{+-}n_- - v_{-+}n_+ \qquad (12.4.2)$$
$$dn_-/dt = v_{-+}n_+ - v_{+-}n_- \qquad (12.4.3)$$

The factors v_{+-} and v_{-+} characterize the probabilities for transfer from seller to buyer and back, respectively

$$v_{+-} = 1/v_{-+} = v \exp(U), \quad U = \alpha p^{-1}dp/dt + \beta(1 - p) \qquad (12.4.4)$$

Price p(t) is given in units of its fundamental value. The first term in the utility function, U, characterizes the "chartist" behavior while the second term describes the "fundamentalist" pattern. The factor v has the sense of the frequency of transitions between seller and buyer behavior. Since $n_+(t) = 1 - n_-(t)$, the system (12.4.1)–(12.4.3) is reduced to the equation

$$dn_+/dt = v_{+-}(1 - n_+) - v_{-+}n_+ \qquad (12.4.5)$$

The price formation equation is assumed to have the following form

$$dp/dt = \gamma D_{ex} \qquad (12.4.6)$$

where the excess demand, D_{ex}, is proportional to the excess number of buyers

$$D_{ex} = \delta(n_+ - n_-) = \delta(2n_+ - 1) \qquad (12.4.7)$$

12.4.2 PRICE-DEMAND RELATIONS

The model described above is defined with two observable variables, $n_+(t)$ and $p(t)$. In equilibrium, its solution is $n_+ = 0.5$ and $p = 1$. The necessary stability condition for this model is

$$\alpha\delta\gamma\nu \leq 1 \qquad (12.4.8)$$

The typical stable solution for this model (relaxation of the initially perturbed values of n_+ and p) is given in Figure 12.1. Lower values of α and γ suppress oscillations and facilitate relaxation of the initial perturbations. Thus, the rise of the "chartist" component in the utility function increases the price volatility. Numerical solutions with the values of α and γ that slightly violate the condition (12.4.8) can lead to the limit cycle providing that the initial conditions are very close to the equilibrium values (see Figure 12.2). Otherwise, violation of the condition (12.4.8) leads to system instability, which can be interpreted as a market crash.

The basic model (12.4.1)–(12.4.7) can be extended in several ways. First, the condition of the constant number of traders (12.4.1)

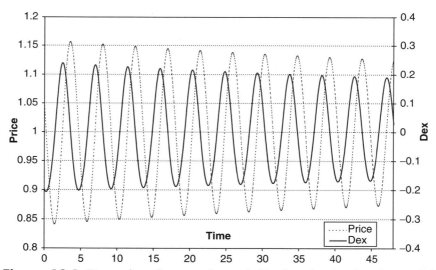

Figure 12.1 Dynamics of excess demand (Dex) and price for the model (12.4.5)–(12.4.7) with $\alpha = \beta = \gamma = 1$, $n_+(0) = 0.4$ and $p(0) = 1.05$.

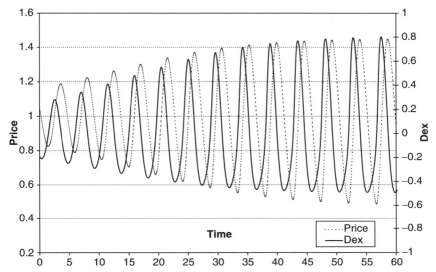

Figure 12.2 Dynamics of excess demand (Dex) and price for the model (12.4.5)–(12.4.7) with $\alpha = 1.05$, $\beta = \gamma = 1$, $n_+(0) = 0.4$ and $p(0) = 1.05$.

can be dropped. The system has three variables (n_+, n_-, p) and therefore may potentially describe deterministic chaos (see Chapter 7). Also, one can randomize the model by adding noise to the utility function (12.4.4) or to the price formation equation (12.4.6). Interestingly, the latter option may lead to a negative correlation between price and excess demand, which is not possible for the deterministic equation (12.4.6) [17].

12.4.3 WHY TECHNICAL TRADING MAY BE SUCCESSFUL

A simple extension of the basic model (12.4.1)–(12.4.7) provides some explanation as to why technical trading may sometimes be successful [18]. Consider a system with a constant number of traders N that consists of "regular" traders N_R and "technical" traders N_T: $N_T + N_R = N = \text{const}$. The "regular" traders are divided into buyers, $N_+(t)$, and sellers, $N_-(t)$: $N_+ + N_- = N_R = \text{const}$. The relative numbers of "regular" traders, $n_+(t) = N_+(t)/N$ and $n_-(t) = N_-(t)/N$, are described with the equations (12.4.2)–(12.4.4). The price formation in equation (12.4.6) is also retained. However, the excess demand, in contrast to (12.4.7), incorporates the "technical" traders

$$D_{ex} = \delta(n_+ - n_- + Fn_T) \qquad (12.4.9)$$

In (12.4.9), $n_T = N_T/N$ and function F is defined by the technical trader strategy. We have chosen a simple technical rule "buying on dips – selling on tops," that is, buying at the moment when the price starts rising, and selling at the moment when price starts falling

$$F(k) = \begin{cases} 1, & p(k) > p(k-1) \text{ and } p(k-1) < p(k-2) \\ -1, & p(k) < p(k-1) \text{ and } p(k-1) > p(k-2) \\ 0, & \text{otherwise} \end{cases} \qquad (12.4.10)$$

Figure 12.3 shows that inclusion of the "technical" traders in the model strengthens the price oscillations. This result can be easily interpreted. If "technical" traders decide that price is going to fall, they sell and thus decrease demand. As a result, price does fall and the "chartist" mood of "regular" traders forces them to sell. This suppresses price further until the "fundamentalist" motivation of

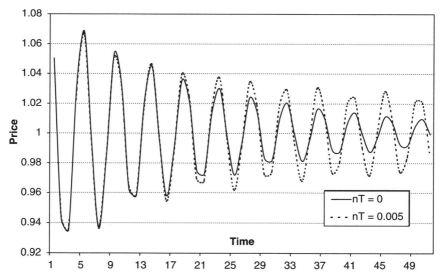

Figure 12.3 Price dynamics for the technical strategy (12.4.10) for $\alpha = \gamma = \delta = \nu = 1$ and $\beta = 4$ with initial conditions $n_+(0) = 0.4$ and $p(0) = 1.05$.

"regular" traders becomes overwhelming. The opposite effect occurs if "technical" traders decide that it is time to buy: they increase demand and price starts to grow until it notably exceeds its fundamental value. Hence, if the "technical" traders are powerful enough in terms of trading volumes, their concerted action can sharply change demand upon "technical" signal. This provokes the "regular" traders to amplify a new trend, which moves price in the direction favorable to the "technical" strategy.

12.4.4 THE BIRTH OF A LIQUID MARKET

Market liquidity implies the presence of traders on both the bid/ask sides of the market. In emergent markets (e.g., new electronic auctions), this may be a matter of concern. To address this problem, the basic model (12.4.1)–(12.4.7) was expanded in the following way [19]

$$dn_+/dt = v_{+-}n_- - v_{-+}n_+ + \Sigma R_{+i} + \rho_+ \qquad (12.4.11)$$

$$dn_-/dt = v_{-+}n_+ - v_{+-}n_- + \Sigma R_{-i} + \rho_- \qquad (12.4.12)$$

The functions $R_{\pm i}(i = 1, 2, \ldots, M)$ and $\rho_\pm$ are the deterministic and stochastic rates of entering and exiting the market, respectively. Let us consider three deterministic effects that define the total number of traders.[6] First, we assume that some traders stop trading immediately after completing a trade as they have limited resources and/or need some time for making new decisions

$$R_{+1} = R_{-1} = -bn_+n_-, \; b > 0 \qquad (12.4.13)$$

Also, we assume that some traders currently present in the market will enter the market again and will possibly bring in some "newcomers." Therefore, the inflow of traders is proportional to the number of traders present in the market

$$R_{+2} = R_{-2} = a(n_+ + n_-), \; a > 0 \qquad (12.4.14)$$

Lastly, we account for "unsatisfied" traders leaving the market. Namely, we assume that those traders who are not able to find the trading counterparts within a reasonable time exit the market

$$R_{+3} = \begin{cases} -c(n_+ - n_-) & \text{if } n_+ > n_- \\ 0, & \text{if } n_+ \leq n_- \end{cases}$$

$$R_{-3} = \begin{cases} -c(n_- - n_+) & \text{if } n_- > n_+ \\ 0, & \text{if } n_- \leq n_+ \end{cases} \qquad (12.4.15)$$

We call the parameter $c > 0$ the "impatience" factor. Here, we neglect the price variation, so that $v_{+-} = v_{-+} = 0$. We also neglect the stochastic rates $\rho_{\pm}$. Let us specify

$$n_+(0) - n_-(0) = \delta > 0. \qquad (12.4.16)$$

Then equations (12.4.11)–(12.4.12) have the following form

$$dn_+/dt = a(n_+ + n_-) - bn_+ n_- - c(n_+ - n_-) \qquad (12.4.17)$$

$$dn_-/dt = a(n_+ + n_-) - bn_+ n_- \qquad (12.4.18)$$

The equation for the total number of traders $n = n_+ + n_-$ has the Riccati form[7]

$$dn/dt = 2an - 0.5bn^2 + 0.5b\delta^2 \exp(-2ct) - c\delta \exp(-ct) \quad (12.4.19)$$

Equation (12.4.19) has the asymptotic solution

$$n_0 = 4a/b \qquad (12.4.20)$$

An example of evolution of the total number of traders (in units of n_0) is shown in Figure 12.4 for different values of the "impatience" factor. Obviously, the higher the "impatience" factor, the deeper the minimum of $n(t)$ will be. At sufficiently high "impatience" factor, the finite-difference solution to equation (12.4.19) falls to zero. This means that the market dies out due to trader impatience. However, the exact solution never reaches zero and always approaches the asymptotic value (12.4.20) after passing the minimum. This demonstrates the drawback of the continuous approach. Indeed, a non-zero number of traders that is lower than unity does not make sense. One way around this problem is to use a threshold, n_{min}, such that

$$n \pm (t) = 0 \text{ if } n \pm (t) < n_{min} \qquad (12.4.21)$$

Still, further analysis shows that the discrete analog of the system (12.4.17)–(12.4.18) may be more adequate than the continuous model [19].[8]

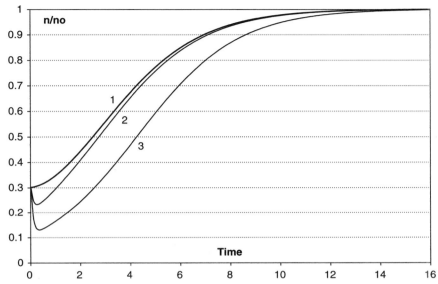

Figure 12.4 Dynamics of the number of traders described with equation (12.4.19) with a = 0.25, b = 1, $n_+(0) = 0.2$, and $n_-(0) = 0.1$: 1 - c = 1; 2 - c = 10; 3 - c = 20.

12.5 REFERENCES FOR FURTHER READING

Reviews [1, 5] and the recent collection [6] might be a good starting point for deeper insight into this quickly evolving field.

12.6 EXERCISES

**1. Discuss the derivation of the GARCH process with the agent-based model [21].

**2. Discuss the insider trading model [22]. How would you model agents having knowledge of upcoming large block trades?

**3. Discuss the parsimony problem in agent-based modeling of financial markets (use [16] as the starting point).

**4. Discuss the agent-based model of business growth [23].

**5. Verify if the model (12.4.1)–(12.4.7) exhibits a price distribution with fat tails.

Comments

CHAPTER 1

1. The author calls this part *academic* primarily because he has difficulty answering the question "So, how can we make some money with this stuff?" Undoubtedly, "money-making" mathematical finance has deep academic roots.
2. Lots of information on the subject can also be found on the websites *http://www.econophysics.org* and *http://www.unifr.ch/econophysics*.
3. Still, Section 7.1 is a useful precursor for Chapter 12.
4. It should be noted that scientific software packages such as Matlab and S-Plus (let alone "in-house" software developed with C/C++) are often used for sophisticated financial data analysis. But Excel, having a wide array of built-in functions and programming capabilities with Visual Basic for Applications (VBA) [13], is ubiquitously employed in the financial industry.

CHAPTER 2

1. In financial literature, return is sometimes defined as $[P(t) - P(t-1)]$ while the variable $R(t)$ in (2.2.1) is named *rate of return*.
2. For the formal definition of IID, see Section 5.1.
3. USD/JPY denotes the price of one USD in units of JPY, etc.
4. Technical analysis is based on the seeking and interpretation of patterns in past prices [7]. Fundamental analysis is evaluation the company's

business quality based on its growth expectations, cash flow, and so on [8].

5. Arbitrage trading strategies are discussed in Section 10.4.

6. An instructive discussion on EMH and rational bubbles is given also on L. Tesfatsion's website: *http://www.econ.iastate.edu/classes/econ308/tesfatsion/emarketh.htm.*

CHAPTER 4

1. In the physical literature, the diffusion coefficient is often defined as $D = kT/(6\pi\eta R)$. Then $E[r^2] - r_0^2 = 6Dt$.
2. The general case of the random walk is discussed in Section 5.1.
3. Here we simplify the notations: $\mu(t) = \mu, \sigma(y(t), t) = \sigma$.
4. The notation $y = O(x)$ means that y and x are of the same asymptotic order, that is, $0 < \lim_{t \to 0} [y(t)/x(t)] < \infty$.

CHAPTER 5

1. See *http://econ.la.psu.edu/~hbierens/EASYREG.HTM.*

CHAPTER 7

1. Ironically, markets may react unexpectedly even at "expected" news. Consider a Federal Reserve interest rate cut, which is an economic stimulus. One may expect market rally after its announcement. However, prices might have already grown in anticipation of this event. Then investors may start immediate profit taking, which leads to falling prices.
2. In the case with $\gamma < 0$, the system has an energy source and the trajectory is an unbounded outward spiral.

CHAPTER 8

1. See, for example, [1] and references therein. Note that the GARCH models generally assume that the unconditional innovations are normal.
2. While several important findings have been reported after publishing [2], I think this conclusion still holds. On a philosophical note, statistical data analysis in general is hardly capable of attaining perfection of mathematical proof. Therefore, scholars with the "hard-science"

background may often be dissatisfied with rigorousness of empirical research.
3. There has been some interesting research on the distribution of the company sizes [3, 4].
4. The foreign exchange data available to academic research are overwhelmingly bank quotes (*indicative rates*) rather than the real inter-bank transaction rates (so-called *firm rates*) [5].

CHAPTER 9

1. In financial literature, derivatives are also called *contingent claims*.
2. The names of the American and European options refer to the exercising rule and are not related to geography. Several other types of options with complicated payoff rules (so-called *exotic options*) have been introduced in recent years [1−3].
3. The U.S. Treasury bills are often used as a benchmark for the risk-free asset.
4. Here and further, the transaction fees are neglected.
5. We might choose also one share and $-\left(\dfrac{\partial F}{\partial S}\right)^{-1}$ options.

CHAPTER 10

1. See Chapter 11.
2. Qualitative graphical presentation of the efficient frontier and the capital market line is similar to the trade-off curve and the trade-off straight line, respectively, depicted in Figure 10.1.
3. Usually, Standard and Poor's 500 Index is used as proxy for the U.S. market portfolio.
4. ROE = E/B where E is earnings; B is the book value that in a nutshell equals the company's assets minus its debt.

CHAPTER 11

1. In risk management, the self-explanatory notion of P/L is used rather than return.
2. In the current literature, the following synonyms of ETL are sometimes used: *expected shortfall* and *conditional VaR* [2].
3. EWMA or GARCH are usually used for the historical volatility forecasts (see Section 4.3).

CHAPTER 12

1. Lots of useful information on agent-based computational economics are present on L. Tesfatsion's website: *http://www.econ.iastate.edu/tesfatsi/ace.htm*. Recent developments in this field can also be found in the materials of the regularly held Workshops on Economics and Heterogeneous Interacting Agents (WEHIA), see, for example, *http://www.nda.ac.jp/cs/AI/wehia04*.

2. I have listed the references to several important models. Early research and recent working papers on the agent-based modeling of financial markets can be found on W. A. Brock's (*http://www.ssc.wisc.edu/~wbrock/*),

   C. Chiarella's (*http://www.business.uts.edu.au/finance/staff/carl.html*),

   J. D. Farmer's (*http://www.santafe.edu/~jdf*),

   B. LeBaron's (*http://people.brandeis.edu/~blebaron/index.htm*),

   T. Lux's (*http://www.bwl.uni-kiel.de/vwlinstitute/gwrp/team/lux.htm*), and

   S. Solomon's (*http://shum.huji.ac.il/~sorin/*) websites.

3. In a more consistent yet computationally demanding formulation, the function f_i depends also on current return ρ_t, that is, $E_i, t[\rho_{t+1}] = f_i(\rho_t, \ldots, \rho_{t-Li})$ [8, 9].

4. Log price in the left-hand side of equation (12.3.7) may be a better choice in order to avoid possible negative price values [12].

5. See also Section 7.1.

6. This model has some similarity with the mating dynamics model where only agents of opposite sex interact and deactivate each other, at least temporarily. In particular, this model could be used for describing attendance of the singles' clubs.

7. Equation (12.4.19) can be transformed into the Schrodinger equation with the Morse-type potential [19].

8. Another interesting example of qualitative difference between the continuous and discrete evolutions of the same system is given in [20].

References

CHAPTER 1

1. J. Y. Campbell, A. W. Lo, and A. C. MacKinlay, *The Econometrics of Financial Markets,* Princeton University Press, 1997.
2. W. H. Green, *Econometric Analysis*, Prentice Hall, 1998.
3. S. R. Pliska, *Introduction to Mathematical Finance: Discrete Time Models,* Blackwell, 1997.
4. S. M. Ross, *Elementary Introduction to Mathematical Finance: Options and Other Topics,* Cambridge University Press, 2002.
5. R. N. Mantegna and H. E. Stanley, *An Introduction in Econophysics: Correlations and Complexity in Finance,* Cambridge University Press, 2000.
6. J. P. Bouchaud and M. Potters, *Theory of Financial Risks: From Statistical Physics to Risk Management,* Cambridge University Press, 2000.
7. M. Levy, H. Levy, and S. Solomon, *The Microscopic Simulation of Financial Markets: From Investor Behavior to Market Phenomena,* Academic Press, 2000.
8. K. Ilinski, *Physics of Finance: Gauge Modeling in Non-Equilibrium Pricing*, Wiley, 2001.
9. J. Voit, *Statistical Mechanics of Financial Markets,* Springer, 2003.
10. D. Sornette, *Why Stock Markets Crash: Critical Events in Complex Financial Systems*, Princeton University Press, 2003.
11. S. Da Silva (Ed), *The Physics of the Open Economy,* Nova Science, 2005.
12. B. LeBaron, "Agent-Based Computational Finance: Suggested Readings and Early Research," *Journal of Economic Dynamics and Control* **24**, 679–702 (2000).

13. M. Jackson and M. Staunton, *Advanced Modeling in Finance Using Excel and VBA,* Wiley, 2001.

CHAPTER 2

1. C. Alexander, *Market Models: A Guide to Financial Data Analysis,* Wiley, 2001.
2. M. M. Dacorogna, R. Gencay, U. Muller, R. B. Olsen, and O. V. Pictet, *An Introduction to High-Frequency Finance,* Academic Press, 2001.
3. See [1.1].
4. T. Lux and D. Sornette: "On Rational Bubbles and Fat Tails," *Journal of Money, Credit, and Banking* **34**, 589-610 (2002).
5. R. C. Merton, *Continuous Time Finance,* Blackwell, 1990.
6. Z. Bodie and R. C. Merton, *Finance,* Prentice Hall, 1998.
7. R. Edwards and J. Magee, *Technical Analysis of Stock Trends,* 8th Ed., AMACOM, 2001.
8. S. Cottle, R. F. Murray, and F. E. Block, *Security Analysis,* McGraw-Hill, 1988.
9. B. G. Malkiel, *A Random Walk Down Wall Street,* Norton, 2003.
10. R. J. Shiller, *Irrational Exuberance,* Princeton University Press, 2000.
11. E. Peters, *Chaos and Order in Capital Markets,* Wiley, 1996.
12. A. W. Lo and A. C. MacKinlay, *A Non-Random Walk Down Wall Street,* Princeton University Press, 1999.
13. See [1.9].
14. D. Kahneman and A. Tversky (Eds.), *Choices, Values and Frames,* Cambridge University Press, 2000.
15. R. H. Thaler (Ed), *Advances in Behavioral Finance,* Russell Sage Foundation, 1993.
16. D. Kahneman and A. Tversky: "Prospect Theory: An Analysis of Decision Under Risk," *Econometrica* **47**, 263-291 (1979). See also [14], pp. 17–43.
17. M. A. H. Dempster and C. M. Jones: "Can Technical Pattern Trading Be Profitably Automated? 1. The Channel; 2. The Head and Shoulders, *Working Papers,* The Judge Institute of Management Studies, University of Cambridge, November and December, 1999.
18. A. W. Lo, H. Mamaysky, and J. Wang: "Foundations of Technical Analysis: Computational Algorithms, Statistical Inference, and Empirical Implementation," *NBER Working Paper W7613,* 2000.
19. B. LeBaron: "Technical Trading Profitability in Foreign Exchange Markets in the 1990s," *Working Paper,* Brandeis University, 2000.
20. R. Clow: "Arbitrage Stung by More Efficient Market," *Financial Times* April 21, 2002.

CHAPTER 3

1. W. Feller, *An Introduction to Probability Theory and Its Applications,* Wiley, 1968.
2. See [1.5].
3. See [1.6].
4. W. H. Press, B. P. Flannery, S. A. Teukolsky, and W. T. Wetterling, *Numerical Recipes: Art of Scientific Programming,* Cambridge University Press, 1992.
5. P. Embrechts, C. Klupperberg, and T. Mikosch, *Modeling External Events for Insurance and Finance,* Springer, 1997.
6. J. P. Nolan, *Stable Distributions,* Springer-Verlag, 2002.
7. B. B. Mandelbrot, *Fractals and Scaling in Finance,* Springer-Verlag, 1997.
8. See [1.9].

CHAPTER 4

1. C. W. Gardiner, *Handbook of Stochastic Methods for Physics, Chemistry, and the Natural Sciences,* Springer-Verlag, 1997.
2. S. N. Neftci, *An Introduction to the Mathematics of Financial Derivatives,* 2nd Ed., Academic Press, 1996.
3. See [1.1].
4. E. Scalas, R. Gorenflo, and F. Mainardi, "Fractional Calculus and Continuous-time Finance," *Physica* **A284**, 376–384, (2000).
5. J. Masoliver, M. Montero, and G. H. Weiss, "A Continuous Time Random Walk Model for Financial Distributions," *Physical Review* **E67**, 21112–21121 (2003).
6. W. Horsthemke and R. Lefevr, *Noise-Induced Transitions. Theory and Applications in Physics, Chemistry, and Biology,* Springer-Verlag, 1984.
7. B. Oksendal: *Stochastic Differential Equations, An Introduction with Applications,* Springer-Verlag, 2000.
8. I. Karatzas and S. E. Shreve, *Brownian Motion and Stochastic Calculus,* Springer-Verlag, 1997.

CHAPTER 5

1. P. H. Franses, *Time Series Models for Business and Economic Forecasting,* Cambridge University Press, 1998.
2. J. D. Hamilton, *Time Series Analysis,* Princeton University Press, 1994.

3. See [2.1].
4. See [1.1].
5. R. Sullivan, A. Timmermann, and H. White: "Data Snooping, Technical Trading Rule Performance, and the Bootstrap," *Journal of Finance* **54**, 1647–1692 (1999).
6. See [1.2].
7. See [2.2].

CHAPTER 6

1. See [2.4].
2. H. O. Peitgen, H. Jurgens, and D. Saupe, *Chaos and Fractals: New Frontiers in Science,* Springer-Verlag, 1992.
3. See [2.11].
4. See [1.1].
5. C. J. G. Evertsz and B. B. Mandelbrot, *Multifractal Measures,* in [2].
6. B. B. Mandelbrot: "Limit Lognormal Multifractal Measures," *Physica* **A163**, 306–315 (1990).

CHAPTER 7

1. B. LeBaron, "Chaos and Nonlinear Forecastability in Economics and Finance," *Philosophical Transactions of the Royal Society of London* **348A**, 397–404 (1994).
2. W. A. Brock, D. Hsieh, and B. LeBaron, *Nonlinear Dynamics, Chaos, and Instability: Statistical Theory and Economic Evidence,* MIT Press, 1991.
3. See [2.11].
4. T. Lux, "The Socio-economic Dynamics of Speculative Markets: Interacting Agents, Chaos, and the Fat Tails of Return Distributions," *Journal of Economic Behavior and Organization* **33**,143–165 (1998).
5. R. C. Hilborn, *Chaos and Nonlinear Dynamics: An Introduction for Scientists and Engineers,* Oxford University Press, 2000.
6. See [2.5].
7. P. Berge, Y. Pomenau, and C. Vidal, *Order Within Chaos: Towards a Deterministic Approach to Turbulence,* Wiley, 1986.
8. J. Gleick, *Chaos: Making New Science,* Penguin, 1988.
9. D. Ruelle, *Chance and Chaos,* Princeton University Press, 1991.
10. See [6.2].

CHAPTER 8

1. See [2.2].
2. See [1.5].
3. K. Okuyama, M. Takayasu, and H. Tajkayasu, "Zipf's Law in Income Distributions of Companies," *Physica* **A269**, 125–131 (1999).
4. R. Axtell, "Zipf Distribution of U.S. Firm Sizes," *Science,* **293**, 1818–1820 (2001).
5. C. A. O. Goodhart and M. O'Hara, "High Frequency Data in Financial Markets: Issues and Applications," *Journal of Empirical Finance* **4**, 73–114 (1997).
6. See [3.7].
7. See [2.11].
8. See [1.1].
9. See [1.6].
10. A. Figueiredo, I. Gleria, R. Matsushita, and S. Da Silva, "Autocorrelation as a Source of Truncated Levy Flights in Foreign Exchange Rates," *Physica* **A323**, 601–625 (2003).
11. P. Gopikrishnan, V. Plerou, L. A. N. Amaral, M. Meyer, and E. H. Stanley, "Scaling of the Distribution of Fluctuations of Financial Market Indices," *Physical Review* **E60**, 5305–5316 (1999).
12. V. Plerou, P. Gopikrishnan, L. A. N. Amaral, M. Meyer, and E. H. Stanley, "Scaling of the Distribution of Price Fluctuations of Individual Companies," *Phys. Rev.* **E60**, 6519–6529 (1999).
13. X. Gabaix, P. Gopikrishnan, V. Plerou, and H. E. Stanley, "A Theory of Power-law Distributions in Financial Market Fluctuations, Nature," **423**, 267–270 (2003).
14. O. Biham, O. Malcai, M. Levy, and S. Solomon, "Generic Emergence of Power-Law Distributions and Levy-Stable Intermittent Fluctuations in Discrete Logistic Systems," *Phys. Rev.* **E58**, 1352–1358 (1998).
15. J. D. Farmer, "Market Force, Ecology, and Evolution," *Working Paper,* Santa Fe Institute, 1998.
16. See [1.10].
17. See [1.9].
18. B. LeBaron, "Stochastic Volatility as a Simple Generator of Apparent Financial Power Laws and Long Memory," *Quantitative Finance* **1**, 621–631 (2001).
19. T. Lux, "Power Laws and Long Memory," *Quantitative Finance* **1**, 560–562 (2001).

20. F. Schmitt, D. Schertzer, and S. Lovejoy, "Multifractal Fluctuations in Finance," *International Journal of Theoretical and Applied Finance* **3**, 361–364 (2000).
21. N. Vandewalle and M. Ausloos, "Multi-Affine Analysis of Typical Currency Exchange Rates," *Eur. Phys. J.* **B4**, 257–261 (1998).
22. B. Mandelbrot, A. Fisher, and L. Calvet, "A Multifractal Model of Asset Returns," *Cowless Foundation Discussion Paper* 1164, 1997.
23. T. Lux, "Turbulence in Financial Markets: The Surprising Explanatory Power of Simple Cascade Models," *Quantitative Finance* **1**, 632–640 (2001).
24. L. Calvet and A. Fisher, "Multifractality in Asset Returns: Theory and Evidence," *Review of Economics and Statistics* **84**, 381–406 (2002).
25. L. Calvet and A. Fisher, "Regime-Switching and the Estimation of Multifractal Processes," *Working Paper,* Harvard University, 2003.
26. T. Lux, "The Multifractal Model of Asset Returns: Its Estimation via GMM and Its Use for Volatility Forecasting," *Working Paper,* University of Kiel, 2003.
27. J. D. Farmer and F. Lillo, "On the Origin of Power-Law Tails in Price Fluctuations," *Quantitative Finance* **4**, C7–C10 (2004).
28. V. Plerou, P. Gopikrishnan, X. Gabaix, and H. E. Stanley, "On the Origin of Power-Law Fluctuations in Stock Prices," *Quantitative Finance* **4**, C11–C15 (2004).
29. P. Weber and B. Rosenow, "Large Stock Price Changes: Volume or Liquidity?" *http://xxx.lanl.gov/cond-mat 0401132.*
30. T. Di Matteo, T. Aste, and M. Dacorogna, "Long-Term Memories of Developed and Emerging Markets: Using the Scaling Analysis to Characterize Their Stage of Development," *http://xxx.lanl.gov/cond-mat 0403681.*

CHAPTER 9

1. J. C. Hull, *Options, Futures, and Other Derivatives,* 3rd Ed., Prentice Hall, 1997.
2. P. Wilmott, *Derivatives: The Theory and Practice of Financial Engineering,* Wiley, 1998.
3. A. Lipton, *Mathematical Methods for Foreign Exchange, A Financial Engineer's Approach,* World Scientific, 2001.
4. See [4.2].
5. F. Black and M. Scholes, "The Pricing of Options and Corporate Liabilities," *Journal of Political Economy* **81**, 637–659 (1973).
6. See [2.5].

7. J. P. Bouchaud, "Welcome to a Non-Black-Scholes World," *Quantitative Finance* **1**, 482–483 (2001).

8. L. Borland, "A Theory of Non-Gaussian Option Pricing," *Quantitative Finance* 2:415–431, 2002.

9. A. B. Schmidt, "True Invariant of an Arbitrage Free Portfolio," *Physica* **320A**, 535–538 (2003).

10. A. Krakovsky, "Pricing Liquidity into Derivatives," *Risk* **12**, 65 (1999).

11. U. Cetin, R. A. Jarrow, and P. Protter: "Liquidity Risk and Arbitrage Pricing Theory," *Working Paper,* Cornell University, 2002.

12. J. Perella, J. M. Porra, M. Montero, and J. Masoliver, "Black-Sholes Option Pricing Within Ito and Stratonovich Conventions." *Physica* **A278**, 260-274 (2000).

CHAPTER 10

1. See [2.6].

2. See [1.1].

3. See [2.5].

4. P. Silvapulle and C. W. J. Granger, "Large Returns, Conditional Correlation and Portfolio Diversification: A-Value-at-Risk Approach," *Quantitative Finance* **1**, 542–551 (2001).

5. D. G. Luenberger, *Investment Science,* Oxford University Press, 1998.

6. R. C. Grinold and R. N. Kahn, *Active Portfolio Management,* McGraw-Hill, 2000.

7. R. Korn, *Optimal Portfolios: Stochastic Models for Optimal Investment and Risk Management in Continuous Time,* World Scientific, 1999.

8. J. G. Nicholas, *Market-Neutral Investing: Long/Short Hedge Fund Strategies,* Bloomberg Press, 2000.

9. J. Conrad and K. Gautam, "An Anatomy of Trading Strategies," *Review of Financial Studies* **11**, 489–519 (1998).

10. E. G. Galev, W. N. Goetzmann, and K. G. Rouwenhorst, "Pairs Trading: Performance of a Relative Value Arbitrage Rule," *NBER Working Paper W7032,* 1999.

11. W. Fung and D. A. Hsieh, "The Risk in Hedge Fund Strategies: Theory and Evidence From Trend Followers," *The Review of Financial Studies* **14**, 313–341 (2001).

12. M. Mitchell and T. Pulvino, "Characteristics of Risk and Return in Risk Arbitrage," *Journal of Finance* **56**, 2135–2176 (2001).

13. S. Hogan, R. Jarrow, and M. Warachka, "Statistical Arbitrage and Market Efficiency," *Working Paper,* Wharton-SMU Research Center, 2003.

14. E. J. Elton, W. Goetzmann, M. J. Gruber, and S. Brown, *Modern Portfolio: Theory and Investment Analysis,* Wiley, 2002.

CHAPTER 11

1. P. Jorion, *Value at Risk: The New Benchmark for Managing Financial Risk,* McGraw-Hill, 2000.
2. K. Dowd, *An Introduction to Market Risk Measurement,* Wiley, 2002.
3. P. Artzner, F. Delbaen, J. M. Eber, and D. Heath, "Coherent Measures of Risk," *Mathematical Finance* **9**, 203–228 (1999).
4. J. Hull and A. White, "Incorporating Volatility Updating into the Historical Simulation Method for Value-at-Risk," *Journal of Risk* **1**, 5–19 (1998).
5. A. J. McNeil and R. Frey, "Estimation of Tail-Related Risk for Heteroscedastic Financial Time Series: An Extreme Value Approach," *Journal of Empirical Finance* **7**, 271–300 (2000).
6. J. A. Lopez, "Regulatory Evaluation of Value-at-risk Models," *Journal of Risk* **1**, 37–64 (1999).

CHAPTER 12

1. See [1.12].
2. D. Challet, A. Chessa, A. Marsili, and Y. C. Chang, "From Minority Games to Real Markets," *Quantitative Finance* **1**, 168–176 (2001).
3. W. B. Arthur, "Inductive Reasoning and Bounded Rationality," *American Economic Review* **84**, 406–411 (1994).
4. A. Beja and M. B. Goldman, "On the Dynamic Behavior of Prices in Disequilibrium," *Journal of Finance* **35**, 235–248 (1980).
5. B. LeBaron, "A Builder's Guide to Agent-Based Markets," *Quantitative Finance* **1**, 254–261 (2001).
6. See [1.11].
7. W. A. Brock and C. H. Hommes, "Heterogeneous Beliefs and Routes to Chaos in a Simple Asset Pricing Model," *Journal of Economic Dynamics and Control* **22**, 1235–1274 (1998).
8. B. LeBaron, W. B. Arthur, and R. Palmer, "The Time Series Properties of an Artificial Stock Market," *Journal of Economic Dynamics and Control* **23**, 1487–1516 (1999).
9. M. Levy, H. Levy, and S. Solomon, "A Macroscopic Model of the Stock Market: Cycles, Booms, and Crashes," *Economics Letters* **45**, 103–111 (1994). See also [1.7].

10. C. Chiarella and X. He, "Asset Pricing and Wealth Dynamics Under Heterogeneous Expectations," *Quantitative Finance* **1**, 509–526 (2001).
11. See [7.4].
12. See [8.15].
13. A. B. Schmidt, "Observable Variables in Agent-Based Modeling of Financial Markets" in [1.11].
14. T. Lux and M. Marchesi, "Scaling and Criticality in a Stochastic Multi-Agent Model of Financial Market," *Nature* **397**, 498–500 (1999).
15. B. LeBaron, "Calibrating an Agent-Based Financial Market to Macroeconomic Time Series," *Working Paper,* Brandeis University, 2002.
16. F. Wagner, "Volatility Cluster and Herding," *Physica* **A322**, 607–619 (2003).
17. A. B. Schmidt, "Modeling the Demand-price Relations in a High-Frequency Foreign Exchange Market," *Physica* **A271**, 507–514 (1999).
18. A. B. Schmidt, "Why Technical Trading May Be Successful: A Lesson From the Agent-Based Modeling," *Physica* **A303**, 185-188 (2002).
19. A. B. Schmidt, "Modeling the Birth of a Liquid Market," *Physica* **A283**, 479–485 (2001).
20. S. Solomon, "Importance of Being Discrete: Life Always Wins on the Surface," *Proceedings of National Academy of Sciences* **97**, 10322–10324 (2000).
21. A. H. Sato and H. Takayasu, "Artificial Market Model Based on Deterministic Agents and Derivation of Limit of GARCH Process," *http://xxx.lanl.gov/cond-mat0109139/.*
22. E. Scalas, S. Cincotti, C. Dose, and M. Raberto, "Fraudulent Agents in an Artificial Financial Market," *http://xxx.lanl.gov/cond-mat0310036.*
23. D. Delli Gatti, C. Di Guilmi, E. Gaffeo, G. Giulioni, M. Gallegati, and A. Palestrini, "A New Approach to Business Fluctuations: Heterogeneous Interacting Agents, Scaling Laws and Financial Fragility," *http://xxx.lanl.gov/cond-mat0312096.*

Answers to Exercises

2.2 (a) \$113.56; (b) \$68.13.

2.4 Borrow 100000 USD to buy 100000/1.7705 GBP. Then buy (100000/1.7705)/0.6694 EUR. Exchange the resulting amount to 1.1914[(100000/1.7705)/0.6694] $\approx$ 100525 USD. Return the loan and enjoy profits of \$525 (minus transaction fees).

3.2 (a) 0.157; (b) 1.645; (c) 1.036

3.4 Since $\alpha X + \beta \sim N(\alpha\mu + \beta, (\alpha\sigma)^2)$, it follows that $C^2 = a^2 + b^2$ and $D = (a + b - C)\mu$.

4.3 $(t) = X(0)\exp(-\mu t) + \sigma \int_0^t \exp[-\mu(t - s)]dW(s)$

5.2 For this process, the AR(2) polynomial (5.1.12) is: $1 - 1.2z + 0.32z^2 = 0$. Since its roots, $z = (1.2 \pm 0.4)/0.64 > 1$, are outside the unit circle, the process is covariance-stationary.

5.3 Linear regression for the dividends in 2000 – 2003 is $D = 1.449 + 0.044n$ (where n is number of years since 2000). Hence the dividend growth is $G = 4.4\%$.

7.1 (a) $X^* = 0.5 \pm\sqrt{0.25 - C}$. Hence there are two fixed points at $C < 0.25$, one fixed point at $C = 0.25$, and none for $C > 0.25$.

   (b) $X_1^* \approx 0.14645$ is attractor with the basin $0 \leq X < X_2^*$ where $X_2^* \approx 0.85355$.

9.1 (a) 1) $c = 2.70$, $p = 0.26$; 2) $c = 0.58$, $p = 2.04$.

   (b) The Black-Scholes option prices do not depend on the stock growth rate (see discussion on the risk-neutral valuation).

9.2 Since the put-call parity is violated, you may sell a call and a T-bill for \$(8 + 98) = \$106. Simultaneously, you buy a share and a put for \$(100

+ 3.50) = \$103.50 to cover your obligations. Then you have profits of \$(106 − 103.50) = \$2.50 (minus transaction fees).

10.1   (a) $E[R] = 0.13$, $\sigma = 0.159$; (b) $E[R] = 0.13$, $\sigma = 0.104$.

10.2   (a) $\beta_A = 1.43$;

      (b)   For $\beta_A = 1.43$, $E[R_A] = 0.083$ according to eq(10.2.1). However, the average return for the given sample of returns is 0.103. Hence CAPM is violated in this case.

10.3 $w_1 = (\beta_{21}\beta_{32} - \beta_{22}\beta_{31})/[\beta_{11}(\beta_{22} - \beta_{32}) + \beta_{21}(\beta_{32} - \beta_{12}) + \beta_{31}(\beta_{12} - \beta_{22})]$, $w_2 = (\beta_{12}\beta_{31} - \beta_{11}\beta_{32})/[\beta_{22}(\beta_{11} - \beta_{31}) + \beta_{12}(\beta_{31} - \beta_{21}) + \beta_{32}(\beta_{21} - \beta_{11})]$.

10.4 $\lambda_1 = [\beta_{22}(R_1 - R_f) - \beta_{12}(R_2 - R_f)]/(\beta_{11}\beta_{22} - \beta_{12}\beta_{21})$, $\lambda_2 = [\beta_{11}(R_2 - R_f) - \beta_{21}(R_1 - R_f)]/(\beta_{11}\beta_{22} - \beta_{12}\beta_{21})$.

11.1   (a) \$136760; (b) \$78959.

Index